# Planning in Reverse

## A Viable Approach to Organizational Leadership

Scott Ballantyne
Beth Berret
Mary Ellen Wells

ROWMAN & LITTLEFIELD EDUCATION

A division of

ROWMAN & LITTLEFIELD PUBLISHERS, INC.

*Lanham • New York • Toronto • Plymouth, UK*

Published by Rowman & Littlefield Education
A division of Rowman & Littlefield Publishers, Inc.
A wholly owned subsidiary of The Rowman & Littlefield Publishing Group, Inc.
4501 Forbes Boulevard, Suite 200, Lanham, Maryland 20706
http://www.rowmaneducation.com

Estover Road, Plymouth PL6 7PY, United Kingdom

British Library Cataloguing in Publication Information Available

**Library of Congress Cataloging-in-Publication Data**
Ballantyne, Scott.
  Planning in reverse : a viable approach to organizational leadership / Scott Ballantyne, Beth Berret, Mary Ellen Wells.
      p. cm.
  Includes bibliographical references.
  ISBN 978-1-60709-792-1 (cloth : alk. paper) — ISBN 978-1-60709-793-8 (pbk. : alk. paper) — ISBN 978-1-60709-794-5 (ebook)
  1. Educational leadership—United States. 2. Organizational change—United States—Management. 3. Strategic planning—United States. 4. School improvement programs—United States. I. Berret, Beth, 1956- II. Wells, Mary Ellen, 1962- III. Title.
  LB2805.B2295 2011
  371.2'07—dc22                                        2010045011

Printed in the United States of America

# Contents

# Part III: Planning in Reverse

# Part IV: Learning in Reverse

# Part V: Reverse Process Planning

# Foreword

$A$ resource like no other. The first that I have seen that incorporates facilities, strategic planning, continuity of leadership, and, most important, the instructional process.

Most of us would be insulted to have our organizations referred to as "Mickey Mouse" operations. But have you ever really stopped to think that such a comparison is one of the greatest compliments that one could get? Writing about the health of an organization, the authors give the Disney Corporation, a well-respected organization, as a classic example—one that is certainly a Mickey Mouse operation but one with vision and a commitment to long-term viability of the organization.

*Planning in Reverse* is one of those reference books that everyone has been looking for but has not had the time to read. I picked this book up as my plane took off and, 2 hours later, was all the way through it. This certainly is an airplane read. In today's times of competing resources of people, time, and money, this resource is the quick answer to some long-term problems that we have all faced.

Being a quick read does not diminish the quality of the content. This is one of the few reference books that I have read that can be immediately implemented with relative low cost or no cost. The solution to facilities issues for those burning the candle at both ends—this is a resource that stands alone. Once you get through the book, you can adapt a variety of its forms to your organization or school system and situation. It really is turnkey.

We have all been through our share of strategic planning sessions, leadership workshops, and facilities master plans and reference manuals. But very few take all those components and integrate them into one of the most innovative concepts that is designed to make organizations more successful by changing how we look at the strategic planning process.

We spend days going through the strategic planning process, ending up with a 5- to 10-year plan that eventually becomes stale if we do not keep it current. If not kept up-to-date, the plan becomes irrelevant due to various conditions, such as economics, technology, and change of leadership. While we cannot alter these conditions, we can control the effect that they have on our organization through the planning-in-reverse process.

This particularly becomes a good resource at a time when organizational leadership is playing musical chairs. It seems that as new leaders come through that swinging door, they think that they need to alter their strategic plans. This resource overcomes that weakness.

Acknowledging that static strategic planning processes usually do not work, this resource becomes even more important. Knowing that, we must move from the current process to a more fluid one—one where planning is altered based on implications of an event or events.

As the writers take you through the process, they give concrete, real-life examples, making the concepts easier to understand and operationalize. Ballantyne, Berret, and Wells use the United States Post Office as an organization that has been adversely affected by change. It failed to understand the affect that e-mail with attachments would have on its operations. Using these types of examples, the authors immerse you in the process.

Of particular relevance to me is that this resource acknowledges that the people in the organization are its most valuable assets. Many of my presentations review the relevance of an organization's staff and the fact that organizations do not accomplish anything.

It is the people that do. You can have the best, most well-planned-out and financed strategic plans, but if it is not supported or moved forward by the people in the organization, then it is doomed to immediate failure. The authors acknowledge the fact that great ideas come from employees at all levels. Further highlighted is the fact that those ideas are not in any one area or department.

Although long-term strategic planning has been the magic mantra for many years, we are only now understanding that long-term viability is more important and that the two are not always synonymous.

After you have read this book, you will wonder how you got along without it.

When the economic crisis started in 2008, many of us knew that we could no longer do business as usual in the educational sector. We are at a time when we have to let go of the past and embrace the "new normal." This will be defined as something different to all of us, but unless we begin moving our organizations to a point of long-term viability, our organizations will not be prepared to meet the needs and differences of the children that walk through our schools' doors.

John D. Musso, CAE, RSBA
Executive Director,
Association of School Business Officials International

*John Musso brings over 30 years of experience to his current position of executive director for ASBO International. Before that, he served as chief financial officer for the District of Columbia Public Schools, which employs over 12,000 employees who serve approximately 60,000 students pre-K–12, operating 167 schools and learning centers.*

# Preface

This book exists for a variety of reasons.

*Because of the "disconnects" that we observed in strategic planning implementation.* While originally targeting the education market, we quickly realized the importance of this process for all entities. The phenomenon of long-term strategic planning ineffectiveness is not limited to public and private school systems or colleges and universities. It is prevalent in all organizational segments.

Quite often the people who are affected the most by strategic plans are often forgotten in the process. To ignore the talents and observations of employees because of their position within the organization is to invite potential failure and frustration into the organization. While there may be some organizations that truly utilize the talents of all stakeholders—primarily, employees—it is not a common practice.

This book was written so that organizations—large and small, private and public, for profit and not for profit school systems or colleges and universities—can implement a process that includes all stakeholders and employees in a meaningful role in planning. It is designed so that all can be engaged in the process and become a part of the organization's long-term viability by providing short-term observations.

*As a supplemental text for strategic management and executive leadership courses.* Many organizations will continue to implement strategic plans. Courses in administration and strategic management should consider adding this book as a supplemental text or, at minimum, place it on the required-reading list. It is important for the future leaders of the organizations that drive our society to understand the importance that change will have regarding viability.

Armed with the planning-in-reverse process, they will more easily embrace change, and their organizations may ultimately remain viable. Entities such as schools, hospitals, not-for-profits, government agencies, and businesses may be intrigued in the interview process when students can competently discuss the impact that change will have on an organization and that they are ready to embrace it through planning in reverse.

*As a supplement to a strategic plan.* For many larger organizations, the elimination of long-term strategic planning is simply not practical. The size and force of the organizations require a more focused approach to allocation of resources. These organizations have departments dedicated to planning and are too complex for the elimination of strategic plans. Planning in reverse may actually have a larger impact on these organizations.

It may be difficult for planners in these large organizations to grasp the impact of events at the service-delivery level. Planning in reverse can be set up so that the planning office receives information relevant to the goals of the strategic plan. This added component of planning may ultimately increase the effectiveness of the office of planning by adjusting the strategic-plan goals utilizing the planning-in-reverse model.

*In lieu of strategic planning.* For many small organizations, the idea of a complex long-term strategic plan is simply beyond the resources of the organization. While general long-term vision is essential for the organization, it may be necessary to adjust services or products, as conditions quickly change. For these organizations, planning in reverse may be the driving component that leads to long-term viability.

It is the small entrepreneur who may benefit the most from planning in reverse in this segment. The very nature of small organizations allows them to react more quickly. While planning in reverse is designed to help large organizations react more quickly to change, it allows small organizations that same opportunity. The opportunity to advantage change in one's favor.

## A SPECIAL NOTE ON IMPLEMENTATION

Implementation of the planning-in-reverse model will vary in the amount of time that it takes, based on the size of the organization. It is a fluid process that can be adjusted as the organization implements it and determines the appropriate adjustments that will improve the organization. We are always interested in suggestions, and we provide a forum to disseminate information regarding the process through our website, http://www .planninginreverse.com.

In addition to user-added suggestions, other tools and suggestions will be listed as they become available. It is essential that the best practices of planning in reverse be shared with us so that future editions of the book include practical implementation recommendations. We look forward to assisting you as your organizations begin to plan in reverse.

## ACKNOWLEDGMENTS

We would like to acknowledge and thank individuals who have helped clarify and support the *Planning in Reverse* book project.

A heartfelt thank-you to our publisher Tom Koerner, who provided invaluable guidance on our first endeavor in getting this book completed. Without his help and guidance, the book would not exist. We look forward to additional projects with Tom.

To John Musso, executive director of ASBO International, who, after agreeing to read the book, offered to write the foreword. His unique experience in all facets of education, from managing academic programming to managing $2 billion in transactions, provided a perspective that could not be matched.

To the research and development committee and the administration of Alvernia University, who provided financial support and encouragement for this book. Without their support, the book may not have been accomplished in the appropriate time frame required by the publisher. Alvernia University continues to be a special place offering unique support to faculty, students, and staff.

To Mark Stitzer, president, and Jim Folk, manager, of ScubaVenture in Sinking Spring, Pennsylvania. As we searched for a ship engine order telegraph (speed controller) to photograph for the cover of the book, Mark offered the use of the replica in his dive shop. It provided the perfect image for *Planning in Reverse* and represents the importance of both forward (ahead) and reverse (astern) in guidance and direction.

To Joseph Yarworth, retired Pennsylvania school superintendent and current professor, for providing critical feedback from the perspective of the K–12 school education. Your critical eye was extremely helpful in clarifying certain sections of the book.

To Michael Jupina, vice president of marketing and communications at Saint Joseph's Hospital in Reading, Pennsylvania, for providing feedback and comments from the health-care perspective. Your explanations on how the health-care field can benefit from this process were appreciated.

To James Boscov in providing the feedback from an entrepreneur's perspective. Boscov has been intimately involved in family retail businesses and in the strategic planning process for organizations and boards. His guidance allowed us to adjust the book so that individuals in business can better understand planning in reverse.

To Charles Broad, retired city police chief and current executive director of the Reading Downtown Improvement District Authority, for providing the perspective of governmental agencies. The encouragement provided regarding the practical use by departments and agencies helped us recognize the general application to sections of organizations.

To Sister Margaret Anne Dougherty, past president of Chatfield College, St. Martin, Ohio, and current associate professor of education, for providing a unique collegiate perspective. As a past administrator holding various positions in several institutions and a current member of faculty, she provided information that was invaluable in the completion of the book. Her assistance is treasured.

To Al Weber, president of Tweed-Weber, Inc., for providing perspective as a professional strategic planner; his advice was extremely useful in completing the final manuscript.

## Special Acknowledgments From Scott Ballantyne

To my wife, Marie, and children, Brandon and Shannon, each of whom provides support and encouragement through all my ideas and projects. Thank you for tolerating my crazy schedules and travels. The joy you bring into my life cannot be measured.

To Harley Caroline, my golden retriever, who loves the Chesapeake Bay as much as I do but sat patiently by my side as I worked on the manuscript.

## Special Acknowledgments From Beth Berret

To my husband, Jim, and children, Lauren, Jimmy, and Emily, who provided endless support and encouragement all the while asking *What next?*

Last but certainly not least, my German shepherd, Bailey, who constantly tossed her ball in my lap as I worked on the book, as a gentle
reminder for me to balance work and play.

## Special Acknowledgments From Mary Ellen Wells

To my husband, Greg, and children, Brian and Abby, who patiently put up
with my writing and editing in the evenings, on weekends, on vacations,
and during other times when they would have preferred that I was doing
something else. I love you all.

# Introduction

Planning in reverse is an innovative concept designed to make organizations more successful by altering the perspective utilized in the strategy process. To fully understand how planning in reverse can help an organization, a review of the current planning process is necessary.

Many organizations develop a long-term strategic plan as a guide for the organization. The strategic plan is developed to keep the organization's leaders focused on long-term goals set in an effort to provide a plan for organizational success. These plans are quite often developed through a time-consuming, resource-intensive, consensus-building process. In the typical strategic planning process, stakeholders—all those who have a vested interest in the organization—are selected to provide input into the process, thereby creating an opportunity for everyone to participate in the future planning of the organization.

Strategic plans are typically designed to cover a period generally ranging from 3 to 5 years. The 3- to 5-year plan then becomes the checkpoint against which all decisions moving forward are measured. This guides the implementation of the goals included in such a plan via the developed objectives. This detail in the plan is necessary to achieve the goals of the strategic plan. In other words, it is this plan that guides an organization through the coming years.

Quite often, however, the plan becomes irrelevant due to changes beyond the control of the organization. These changes can be societal, technological, or structural. When such changes occur, a dangerous situation can develop within an organization. Those who bought into the original long-term strategic plan and planning process may feel an obligation to continue to move the plan to its fruition regardless of any conditional change that impedes potential success.

This situation can result in entrenched stakeholders unwilling to adapt to current economic and environmental factors affecting the organization, and as this plan continues to be implemented, the demise of the organization may develop. The changing environmental factors may mean that the services or products that the organization delivers may no longer be needed due to insufficient demand. In addition, changes can impede quality, making the product or service irrelevant. How can societal, technological, or structural changes make a product or service irrelevant?

As you read this book and begin to understand the implications of change, individual examples or ideas that need attention regarding your organization may strike you. It is important to record these items so that they can be later tested to determine how the planning-in-reverse process could have helped avert any negative implications that resulted from these items. These examples can be planned in reverse and developed into a more meaningful example in your organization during implementation. For instance, the following example demonstrates how a societal change affected an organization in a particular sector.

Our society has shifted its belief over time from one that acknowledges that a high school degree is sufficient preparation for a productive and successful life to one in which graduation from college is necessary. This shift in belief reflects a perception of education that has caused a great change in the higher education field. A look at the percentage of high school graduates who plan on attending an institution of higher education has dramatically increased in the recent past.

In the 2008 study by the National Center for Education Statistics, 79% of seniors who graduated in 2004 planned to continue their education in postsecondary institutions, compared to 59% of graduating seniors who planned to continue their education in 1972.[1] As the percentage of students demanding higher education increased, a corresponding increase was called for in the student services designed to help them succeed.

Institutions who failed to address this societal change struggled to continue in operation. Such organizations may have had strategic plans in place that did not include adaptations for such societal change, or they may not have had strategic plans at all. In either case, failing institutions were those that lacked available processes to adapt to the current societal change in a timely manner.

Technological change can also have a dramatic effect on the viability of an organization. An example of this can be seen in print media. As communication devices become more sophisticated, thereby blending communications and information-seeking into one device, the viability of print media continues to face challenges. Individuals today can access information on a real-time basis, thereby reducing the viability of traditional print media.

As these devices continue to develop, the print media organizations that fail to change may face extinction. Evidence of this change already exists, as seen in 2009 with the demise of the *Rocky Mountain News*, in Denver, Colorado. A similar situation occurred in Philadelphia with the financial problems experienced by the holding company that owns the *Philadelphia Inquirer* and the *Daily News*.

Finally, a structural change can be seen in the field of education. In certain geographic locations, the number of parents who have chosen to have their children educated outside of the traditional public or private school has aggressively increased in recent years. Burke[2] cited a 74% growth rate in parents' homeschooling their children since 1999. This acceleration is in part due to the development of cyber schools that accept public funds on behalf of their students. This structural change allows parents the opportunity to stay at home as they would have when homeschooling. The benefit is that these parents who may not have had the expertise to address the educational requirements of their children can now access the expertise while keeping their children from attending school outside of their control.

The preceding three examples provide some insight into the necessity for planning in reverse. To recognize change and its effect on an organization, the thought process regarding long-term strategic planning needs to be substantially altered or even eliminated. To succeed in providing quality services or products—whether they are educational content or government or private services or products—organizations must plan differently than they did in the past.

The necessity of adaptability to changing circumstances addressed by planning in reverse does not mean that long-term viability is not desired.

The long-term health of an organization is exactly the reason for changing. What is necessary is to move from a long-term planning process to
a process that can help its leaders respond to change that may have been
unforeseen at the time that the original plan was developed. Further com-
pounding the problem is the belief that the rate of change is increasing
exponentially, thereby guaranteeing that long-term traditional plans will
be outdated upon their adoption.

Further evidence of this phenomenon is apparent in the thoughts presented by Ray Kurzweil, who indicated that the rate of change is increasing exponentially and that the 21st century will be equivalent to 20,000
years of progress at today's rate.[3] Take, for example, the United States
Post Office adding fax centers to their list of customer services in 1989.

The long-term plan was to add yet another service, thereby increasing
revenue by contracting with a private company to rent space and share fax
fees. What was unpredicted at the time was the surge in e-mail and other
Internet resources, including the ability to easily scan documents and send
via e-mail, which outdated the fax service shortly after it was instituted.

What is needed for organizations to thrive in this new environment of
change and uncertainty is a viable approach to organizational leadership.
In this book, the tools and concepts regarding planning in reverse are provided so that any organization or department will be able to implement
the planning-in-reverse process to provide opportunities to recognize the
impact that a single event may have on an organization.

Planning in reverse will require all individuals in an organization to
understand a new process of thinking, and those individuals need to be
willing to utilize the tools and concepts to evaluate the impact of change
on the organization.

The planning-in-reverse process involves the identification of events as
*implications*. These implications are then classified into *impacts*. These
impacts are further delineated into *external* or *internal*. These impacts are
then evaluated to determine if they are improvements or impediments to
success. Once these events are classified, they are reverse-processed to
determine the potential impact on the organization.

After the impact is assessed, the itemized action plan is developed,
vetted, and submitted for implementation. Integration is the next step in
planning in reverse. It requires leadership to begin to develop the steps
necessary to make appropriate adjustments to ensure that implementation

goes smoothly by bringing all affected parties up to date on the plan. Finally, initiation is the step wherein the adjustments are incorporated into the operation. In using this new process, organizations will become keenly aware of the impact that even minor changes in society can have on their viability or relevance.

This planning-in-reverse process is unique in that it will work in any organization whether it provides educational services, government services, private sector services, or the production of products. This system is of particular importance to the small organization that does not have the resources to overcome potential missteps.

Planning in reverse suggests that long-term static strategic planning will continue to become less and less helpful and that it may ultimately need to be completely replaced by the planning-in-reverse process for organizations to survive. Many large, well-known companies and organizations have failed even though they had long-term strategic plans. These observations indicate a need for a fundamental change in the planning process, thereby suggesting that it is time for planning in reverse.

## NOTES

1. S. J. Ingels, B. W. Dalton, and L. LoGerfo, *Trends Among High School Seniors 1972–2004* (National Center for Education Statistics, 2008).

2. L. M. Burke, "Homeschooling Sees Dramatic Rise in Popularity," January 28, 2009, http://www.heritage.org/research/eduation/wm2254.cfm.

3. R. Kurzweil and C. Meyer, "Understanding the Accelerating Rate of Change," 2003, http//www.kurzweilai.net/articles/art0563.htm.

# Part I

SHORT-TERM LEADERSHIP FOR
LONG-TERM VIABILITY

# 1

## Short-Term Leadership for Long-Term Viability

To change from a long-term strategic planning process to the planning-in-reverse (PIR) process, it is necessary to understand the entire PIR process. The issue that is most important to understand is the need for a departure from traditional static planning to a more fluid process where planning is altered based on implications of a particular event or events.

To understand why a change is necessary, it is important to review the reasons why the current planning process is not working and therefore requires change. Following the description of the rationale for change, a detailed example is provided to illustrate that rationale. As the process is described throughout the book, a better understanding of implementation of the PIR process will reveal itself. Once an organization converts to the PIR method, a fundamental change will occur in its planning process.

Change is a constant unknown. For humans to believe that they can function, order is necessary in their lives. This phenomenon has caused the development of the long-term strategic planning process. It was thought that this planning process would make sense of chaos and allow organizations to prosper in their respective fields. This process then posits the thought that long-term strategic planning will thereby ensure the viability of organizations that take it seriously.

According to organizational theory, the first step in the strategic planning process is to develop long-term strategic plans by identifying key individuals. The test of this exemplar is whether or not it is a fallacy of long-term strategic planning that individuals can accurately predict changes that will occur in society. In other words, are organizations successful only if they have long-term strategic plans? Conversely, are the organizations that fail, organizations that neglected to complete a strategic plan? Or does the presence or absence of a strategic plan have little impact when significant changes occur that affect an organization?

The answer to the first two questions is no, while the answer to the third gives rise to the need for the PIR process. Organizations succeed and fail due to a variety of factors that influence their viability. These successes and failures, more often than not, revolve around change. For most organizations, change in one or more of a variety of areas is the reason for success or failure. Organizations that are successful quite often reach success due to change that is not encompassed in their strategic plans. Sometimes that change is made internal to the organization, while other times it is external change that causes its success.

Conversely, an organization with a long-term strategic plan may fail because of unfortunate changes to its product or service, negative changes in the market, or societal changes rendering its product undesirable. Regardless of whether a long-term strategic plan is in place or not, it is believed that the fundamental driving force in organizational success or failure is . . . change! This concept suggests that change needs to be harnessed, and this is the reason why *Planning in Reverse* was written. A review of an example of both positive and negative outcomes due to change are provided. In addition, internal and external examples are mentioned.

Events are highlighted in these examples so that the unpredictability of change can be clearly seen. An understanding of these examples provides the blueprint for moving forward in switching your organization to the PIR process so that individual organizations can have better control over their long-term viability. The first example is of an organization familiar to everyone living in the United States.

The United States Postal Service is an organization that has been adversely affected by change. As one continues to evaluate the postal service for its ability to adapt and prosper as technological changes have occurred, it becomes obvious that a failure has occurred. The postal service needed to recognize that e-mail with attachments would severely curtail the amount of quality first-class mail that would be processed in the United States. This potential reduction of mail may have been seen early enough to adjust postal service operations had the post office implemented PIR in its planning department.

Competition may not have been historically considered a threat to the post office because of the possible belief that no competitor would want to deliver a piece of mail 1,000 miles away for 44 cents. Perhaps the post office underestimated the ability of its competitors. United Parcel Service and Federal Express designed systems to compete with the postal service in the area of lucrative package delivery.

In addition, time-sensitive material could be delivered at a premium. This surgical slicing of the profitable segments of the postal service puts increased financial pressure on the remaining postal service, quite often directly on the least profitable section. In other words, that part of the service that is difficult to make a profit on is the only avenue left for the post office to provide service.

These two examples of events that occurred have caused the postal service to decline in efficient operations and caused a stress on its financial operations. These two events may not have been included in its strategic plan, because the plan was constructed before the existence and recognition of these events. In the United States Postal Service, PIR was needed. In a subsequent chapter, the PIR process is explained utilizing a similar example in the education field. This provides an opportunity to view how the PIR system can be applied to any organization.

The post office is now forced to react to the declining revenue balance by raising stamp prices and potentially cutting services, neither of which is a popular choice with the Postal Regulatory Commission. The commission was created by the Postal Service Reorganization Act of 1970 to act as an independent watchdog agency over the United States Postal Service.[1]

Strengthened by the Postal Accountability and Enhancement Act in 2006, the commission was given the authority to set postal rates and conduct public on-the-record hearings concerning proposed rate, mail classification, or major service changes. It also develops and maintains regulations for a modern system of rate regulation, consults with the United States Postal Service on delivery service standards and performance measures, consults with the Department of State on international postal policies, prevents anticompetitive postal practices, promotes transparency and accountability of the postal service as a whole, and resolves complaints.[2]

Opponents of PIR might identify the red tape of a government regulatory agency and unionized workforce as stifling change in the United
States Postal Service. However, the Postal Regulatory Commission is not
unlike similar hierarchical management structures, with the United Parcel
Service and Federal Express each having its own Board of Directors. The
two entities profitably exist with unions and with red tape associated with
regulatory agencies.

Given the fact that the Postal Regulatory Commission was charged to
investigate major postal service changes, proponents of PIR would indicate that PIR could aide in this situation by providing a mechanism for
immediately recognizing the impact that technology affords the consumer
and enabling a reaction that might include enhancing shipping services
and reducing mail delivery after implementation of PIR.

Sticking with an initial strategic plan in the face of a changing situation
and reacting to the competition's enhanced services after the fact—as the
United States Postal Service did in this situation—opened the door for
competitors' success. Different outcomes may have been achieved had
PIR been available.

The 2009 United States Postal Service annual report states that total
mail volume declined 13%, or 25 billion pieces, compared to 2008.[3] The
report also states that operating revenues declined 9.1% to $68 billion.[4]
These volume and revenue decreases are similar to but not quite as large
as the decreases identified in the 2008 annual report. The future does not
look bright for the United States Postal Service.

The Boston Consulting Group, McKinsey, and Accenture—three of the
most reputable consulting firms in the business—project significant volume declines through 2020.[5] The United States Postal Service's response
has been simply to raise rates and reduce services . . . again.

Let us take a look at the United States Postal Service's competitors'
response to current economic woes. The United Parcel Service's major
domestic competitors in the ground parcel delivery service are the United
States Postal Service and Federal Express. As online purchasing continues
to increase, domestic carriers that serve a small specialized section of the
market have emerged in segmented markets. While they are not major
competitors, they are competitors just the same. United Parcel Service did
experience package volume declines in the United States of 2% in 2008,
but overall revenue increased 5% from 2007.[6]

Working with a unionized workforce as heavily regulated as the United States Postal Service, United Parcel Service's 2008 annual report states that the service "strives to increase domestic revenue through cross-selling services to our large and diverse customer base, to control costs through effective network modification and limited expense growth, and to employ technology-driven efficiencies to increase operating profit."[7]

The United Parcel Service plans to use outsourcing, when appropriate, and to continue to use technology to enhance employee productivity and vehicle performance (by reducing fuel consumption), as well as a system to monitor the benefits of the technology. Rate increases, closing of facilities, laying off of employees, and reduction of customer services are not viable options for long-term competitive sustainability at the United Parcel Service.

According to the 2007 Federal Express annual report, its experiences were much the same as at United Parcel Service. Federal Express, even though experiencing a decline in volume, continued to enhance technology, add new hubs, and add additional direct routing to stay attractive to its customers.[8]

Clearly, successful companies such as United Parcel Service and Federal Express are adjusting their strategies based on current events and conditions, whereas struggling organizations such as the United States Postal Service seem to stick with their older strategic plans rather than adjust to new conditions and events, which results in decreased success. The following chapters illustrate how PIR could help schools, universities, businesses, not-for-profits, and governmental agencies (including the United States Postal Service) that are experiencing conditions that are resulting in decreased viability.

## NOTES

1. "Postal Regulatory Commission Strategic and Operational Plan 2008 through 2010," http://www.prc.gov/PRC-DOCS/home/main_nav/StrategicPlan.pdf, 4.
2. "Postal Regulatory Commission Strategic Plan."
3. "The Challenge to Deliver: Creating the 21st Century Postal Service: 2009 USPS Annual Report," http://www.usps.com/financials/_pdf/annual_report_2009.pdf, 4.

4. "2009 USPS Annual Report."

5. "Keynote Address by John E. Potter, Postmaster General and Chief Executive Officer, U.S. Postal Service 2010 National Postal Forum," April 12, 2010, http://www.usps.com/communications/newsroom/speeches/2010/pr10 _pmg_0412.htm.

6. "Resilience: 2008 UPS Annual Report," http://phx.corporate-ir.net/External .File?item=UGFyZW50SUQ9MjA2MTB8Q2hpbGRJRD0tMXxUeXBlPTM =&t=1.

7. "2008 UPS Annual Report."

8. http://www.fedex.com.

# 2

## The Pathway to Long-Term Viability

The pathway to long-term viability involves the participation of all members of the organization. The PIR process relies on the abilities of the employees to begin to recognize events that may have an impact on the organization. The need for the PIR process to include employees also requires that the leaders of the organization listen to the employees with regard to their event scans. Finally, as with any plan, resources are required. While the resources include some funding for supplies, the greatest resource required is employee time.

The success of PIR requires the staff of an organization to play an important role in analyzing internal and external events that may have an impact on such organization. To implement the PIR process, a pathway for communication must be created. Simply stated, a communications process needs to be implemented so that employee scans can be logged and evaluated.

This communication process can most easily be accomplished through the use of dedicated storage space on a web portal or computer. PIR scans by employees can then be stored electronically until the designated time when the scan is evaluated. Once it is evaluated and determined that it is an *implication*, then it can be staged for further assessment.

If it is determined that it is not an implication, the scan may be discarded to save storage space. As the implication moves through the PIR process, it can be further refined as an *impact*, which is either external or internal. It is then evaluated to determine if it is an *improvement* or *impediment* and so ultimately have the itemized action plan developed for *integration* and *initiation* into the organization. The PIR process is triggered by employees of the organization or other interested stakeholders; therefore, employees and leaders need to be trained on how to complete the necessary PIR scans.

Employees are an organization's most valuable asset. Without employees, executing business plans, fulfilling orders, providing services, and producing goods organizations would not exist. Employees are oftentimes looked at as a cog in the machinery. This sometimes allows managers to forget that each employee has ideas based on his or her specific talents. These talents may or may not be utilized in employees' current positions. PIR begins when employees are able to utilize their talents to improve the organization, regardless of their positions.

Employees are oftentimes thought of as being one-dimensional. A great example of this is seen when a group of coworkers go to lunch or dinner together. If individuals at the lunch table include people from sales, customer service, production, and accounting, the accountant will most often be stuck calculating what each employee owes for his or her meal.

The assumption is that because the individual is from the accounting office, he or she is best suited to complete the task. In other words, the folks at the table recognize the special skill that an individual has regarding finance but may be so focused on that skill that they fail to recognize that the accountant likely has additional skills that can be utilized in the organization.

This is also seen when teachers get together to go on a field trip. If they are on a trip to New York City, the English and math teachers will quite often ask the history teacher about the historic architecture of the city. Regardless of the level of knowledge that the teacher may have about New York architectural history, he or she is considered the expert.

In PIR, those same assumptions are apparent with respect to scans. Each individual has an area of expertise, and individuals tend to evaluate events from their own perspectives. Part of this perspective is from their formal education, and part is from their practical experience. This knowledge of employee perspective is valuable when completing and evaluating PIR scans. Individuals associated with the organization need to utilize their talents and backgrounds, not just the skills associated with their positions, to tease out potential implications.

Hidden talents need to be developed and known by organizational leadership. Employees have interests beyond the skill sets required to perform their positions well. For instance, you may have an individual in the legal department who is an avid boater on the Chesapeake Bay. His or her interest in the Chesapeake Bay may not provide additional value to the organization when he or she is performing the duties assigned to the position. It may, however, provide enormous benefits when completing a PIR scan. In keeping with our bay example, think about the following example.

Consider an individual who is working in the legal department of a chicken processor on the eastern shore of Maryland and is reviewing new regulations regarding field runoff into the Chesapeake Bay. Remember that our employee is an avid Chesapeake Bay boater. As a PIR scanning activity, it might be extremely helpful if the employee's area of interest includes the health and history of the Chesapeake Bay.

It might help the organization understand the new regulations and why they were put in place. This information may help create an understanding to develop a new way to control runoff because of the internal knowledge regarding the loss of fishing productivity from the increased nitrogen levels entering the bay.

As is the case with this example, the PIR process requires a thorough understanding of the talents associated with all employees' positions within the organization as well as their outside interests. Part of the time spent on the PIR process will need to be the sharing and understanding of the talents of its employees, including hobbies and interests away from their work environment.

To understand the talents and interests of the organization's employees, listening has to become an organizational priority. How many individuals have been interrupted while answering a question? While hearing is a physical activity, listening is a skill. One can learn to improve his or her listening skills through assessment and practice.

However, listening is a difficult skill to learn because it requires individuals to hear (listen to every word that an individual is saying), understand, and respond. Listening requires patience, and it cannot occur if individuals are formulating a response before the statement is completed. Listening is a skill that needs to be practiced so that it can be implemented as a technique in the PIR process.

The first step in developing this important organizational skill is to assess the level of listening currently exhibited by employees. This step can be introduced as an individual exercise or as a group activity at minimal expense for the organization. One effective assessment tool is taped role-playing. How many times do interruptions occur in conversation? Do employees finish their thoughts? Are there reflective questions challenging or rationalizing ideas? Are employees "there"?

Employees at the Pike Place Fish Market realized early in their careers that they needed to "be present" for their customers.[1] That meant listening with a mind focused on that customer, at that time. This approach aids in the customers' perception that they are number one and that their questions, concerns, and so on, are valued. Such an approach is inclusive and not evaluative. All customers feel valued, not judged.

Once assessment is complete, then the rebuilding or development of advanced listening skills can occur. Listening well is more than simply not interrupting someone. It is also about body language and improved interpersonal relations. If the point of the practice is that in the end, productivity will improve, then rapport with coworkers, supervisors, customers, and students will improve, and assignments will be clearer because of a better understanding of what is expected. It is clear that the development of good listening skills is beneficial to the organization and involves clear and concise speaking, body language that is engaging, and a focused mind.

The ability to change enables travel along the pathway to long-term viability. Human beings are creatures of habit. It is important to recognize that change is difficult for us. Human beings love routine and order; change disrupts. It takes a leap of faith to be willing to alter a process that may have worked for years, because of an event that might develop in the near future. The ability to embrace change and to accept constant adjustment is necessary to be viable. It is a skill that needs to be developed and embraced for PIR to work in an organization.

Organizations introducing change need to recognize that the more that employees are included in the process of change, the more likely they are to accept the outcome. Any and all resistance to change should be openly identified and addressed.

If employees are verbally resistant, with phrases such as "We've always done it that way" or "If it ain't broke, don't fix it"—then resistance is evident. Silent resistance manifests itself in lower productivity, lapses in quality, and absenteeism and so results in a miserable organizational climate. Silent resistance is much more difficult to identify, let alone address, than outright refusal to change. Including those in the process who protest change may at first seem to put a black cloud over the process, but once the change is accepted, the process of change is shared on the employees' terms to others in the organization.

Kurt Lewin's three-stage change model has become classic reading in organizational development courses. Lewin theorized that this model, known as the unfreezing–change–refreeze model, requires the rejection of prior learning as replaced with new behaviors that become habitual.[2] Some employees, however, have been through the model over and over again since the beginning of their careers, often with no opportunity to experience the benefit of the upside of change. But as long as employees understand the result, reoccurring change is easier to tolerate. Take, for example, the introduction of computers in the workplace. There are those who did not see the benefit of computers and believed that "the machine" would be a phase.

At the time, the misunderstanding of change and employee–employer expectations may have ended in termination of the employee not willing to change or not understanding the impact. Therein lies a premise of Lewin's model: For change to progress, one must move past possible anxieties. The way to do that is through education and the elimination of assumptions. Involve employees in the process and assist them in recognizing that just as software needs updating, so too does the workplace.

For these reasons, it is important for change to become the routine. Change has to become the expected rather than the feared so that it can become the routine and therefore feel comfortable for every employee within the organization. As change is implemented, employees will realize that it is not necessarily bad or good; it is simply a part of the job. At the point at which this transformation occurs, PIR can be fully embraced, and the benefits will intensify.

Resources are an integral part of the PIR process. For PIR to be implemented, resources need to be allocated. The financial commitment for the PIR process can be altered to fit the size of the organization. PIR will not work if sufficient time—the most important resource—is not allocated to the entire process. The amount of time and dedication by each employee will vary depending on his or her position within the PIR process. As with any planning model, the more directly an employee is connected to planning in an organization, the greater the amount of resources required.

Many individuals will be able to effectively participate in the PIR process, with minimal amounts of time being utilized. This is the beauty of PIR. Employees who provide initial scans are providing meaningful information that ultimately helps define the pathway to long-term viability without requiring a significant resource allocation of time. Other employees involved in the evaluation phase will more likely require more significant allotments of time for the process.

Take Southwest Airlines, for example. In the book *Nuts*, Herb Kelleher readily identifies employees as the heart of the organization.[3] Change is culturally anticipated at Southwest Airlines as a means to maintain quality and competitiveness. Ideas are embraced from all employees, regardless of their position in the organization. At Southwest, employees are people too and those who care, listen—which includes everyone!

Employees who are closest to the product or the process are more likely to recognize, before those in upper-level management positions, that change is required. The line employees, given the right culture and the recognition that employees are people too, are organizations' most valuable resources in a time of competitive change. Complex calculations to reward employees who make contributions to organizational success are simply not required when the culture of change in the organization is in place. The PIR process is not about large monetary commitments; it is about recognizing and using resources that may already be in place. Additional resources that will be needed may already be available and so include a meeting room or conference area, as well as dedicated space on a web portal, server, or computer. Think of this as replacing the suggestion box. The web portal is the preferred method of data collection, communication, and storage because of its ease of access from remote locations. These remote locations include alternative work sites, employee homes, and office areas. Access can be set up so that employees can monitor the progress of their submitted scan. Let us not forget that someone should be assigned the task of recognizing that the submitted scan was received, that it is being reviewed, and that $X$ is the time frame.

One way to disrupt this process is not to acknowledge that initial step in the communication phase. Indefinite time frames are not embraced by employees. Without a specific time frame, tasks tend to not be accomplished. The second-easiest way to disrupt the process is if the person responsible to respond does not. If a time frame is given and a response is to be given in $X$ number of days, then there should absolutely be a response in $X$ number of days. Communication at all levels of the organization is important.

For PIR to be successful, a transparent communication pathway must be established and embraced by leadership so that each employee can see value in his or her investment in the organization. To establish the communication pathway allows for full implementation of PIR.

## NOTES

1. Stephen Lundin, Harry Paul, and John Christensen, *Fish* (Hyperion, 2000).

2. Pamela Lewis, Stephen Goodman, Patricia Fandt, and Joseph Michlitsch, *Management Challenges for Tomorrow's Leaders* (Thomson SouthWestern, 2007), 277.

3. Kevin Freiberg and Jackie Freiberg, *Nuts* (Bard Press, 1996).

# 3

## The New Leadership Skill Set Necessary for Today's Business Environment

Leadership necessary to maintain long-term viability in organizations today may look substantially different from yesterday. Society continues to change at an ever-increasing pace. This rapid escalation of the rate of change requires a different set of leadership skills than what may have been seen just 20 years ago.

In addition, organizations are now employing a workforce consisting of the new, technologically advanced graduates of today. These new workers think differently from those of the baby boom generation. When these phenomena are coupled with the new era of globalization, it is no surprise that a new skill set is required for organizations to achieve long-term viability.

Take, for example, Generation X, or those born between 1960 and 1980. During those years, kids witnessed their parents being laid off, rising divorce rates, and technology as a work tool and a force of play. They often were on their own as self-reliant latchkey kids. Disappointment or disillusionment with life, coupled with self-reliance, often results in the feeling for a need to have a plan B. Unlike prior generations, which often stayed bound to the organization that hired them for their first job, Generation X individuals are typically perceived as not remaining loyal to the organization.[1]

Generation X'ers are on the move. They are highly educated, accepting of diverse situations, and technologically sophisticated. They entered the workforce decisive, self-reliant, confident, educated, tolerant of diversity, familiar with a global workplace, loyal to one another rather than the organization, and ready to move on if the mood hit.[2] Generation X'ers like feedback and a recognition that they are equals with their older peers.

The baby boomers were taught to respect elders; the Generation X'ers, to challenge them. The new skill set seems to involve a requirement that respect is earned, regardless of age. Communication skills are necessary—engagement and feedback, individuality, and especially, listening. As originally indicated in the aforementioned communication discussion, Generation X'ers want more than just to be heard; they expect a response, a sincere response.[3]

To make the workplace environment even more complex, add the impact of Generation Y employees, or those born between 1980 and 2002. Technologically savvy, this generation wants to be managed by what they know. Communication—immediate and often via technology—is essential. Generation Y's can easily use the technology to talk with others around the world at the stroke of a key.[4]

They accept the workplace as being already diverse—looking for input and finding solutions from those of different genders, nationality, races, ethnicities, and religious groups—but this generation wants a work–life balance more so than Generation X. Generation Y's really do want successful careers and happy families.[5] Organizations need to investigate the creative workplace. Forget structured hours, formal dress, and all the stereotypes in between. Consider instead in-house social networking sites and peer feedback systems as a means for constant communication and updates.[6]

Complexity is the new norm for organizations as four generations inhabit today's workplace: traditionalists, baby boomers, Generation Xer's, and Generation Y's. Each group has its own strengths and challenges— with different communication styles, expectations, educational levels, and technological expertise—and they all must work together. No longer do the oldest of the generations hold the highest positions and therefore become the most respected. Many times, the workplace is team oriented with the four generations working together. One thing is certain: The old school command-and-control management systems will not work.

Tolerating, even accepting, the difference in the way the groups approach work is a way to overcome a major hurdle. For example, traditionalists and baby boomers are part of a generation that traditionally worked in offices. They feel comfortable interacting with others face-to-face and maintaining schedules. Generation X'ers and Y's have transitioned into road warriors. Their interaction is via a BlackBerry, cell phone, laptop, or even "face-to-face" with the assistance of a video device (e.g., Skype or Wimba). These methods all allow for multiple tasks to be addressed at the same time.[7]

The rate of change in organizations has increased exponentially and will continue to change with increasing speed as technology continues to be the driving force. One fact remains the same: Enhanced communication systems, constant feedback, and a more flexible work environment accepting of a personal–professional balance are requirements for a successful organization.[8]

While some of the skills required for leaders are consistent with prior work on leadership, PIR sees a need to change the delivery of the skill set. PIR is a model that is reactive and that therefore requires leaders who are reactive and bold in their decision making and see the value in being reactive. To maintain viability, these leaders need to make decisions after appropriate assessment. To make an accurate assessment and move in a positive direction, the following skills are required.

Agility, which combines flexibility and speed, is an important skill needed in today's organization. Agility is required because of the rate of change and the new employee mind-set. As subtle changes occur in the population that your organization serves, changes need to be made to the services offered. Without agility as a skill that is embraced, organizations may fail.

Trust and delegation need to be enhanced and practiced in a PIR environment. The premise of PIR is that all employees can spot signals of a future potential implication for the organization. If organizational leaders are requesting that employees be part of the commitment to long-term viability through this process, then leaders must be willing to freely delegate (and reward) assignments and tasks to employees.

There is simply no room for micromanagers in the PIR process. Managers need to delegate the assignments, provide support when necessary, and trust the work when completed. Building trust through mutual respect will be the by-product of PIR.

Decision making is a skill not often practiced or taught. In PIR, decision making is completed through the entire PIR process. This skill set may need to be retaught so that decision making can be made at the appropriate level. Exercises to develop decision-making skills may be necessary in an organization that had previously utilized a central decision-making model. Depending on the size of the organization, this task may need to be started before the implementation of PIR.

*Criticism to enhance* is our term to indicate the importance of self-reflection as well as external review. It is important in the PIR process to continually learn from the process. This includes self-reflective evaluation where an individual leader evaluates his or her performance and decision making with respect to an implication.

Individuals engaged at all levels of the PIR process need to self-reflect on their own decision making with regard to an observation. Additionally, external review needs to become a healthy part of the process. In other words, the PIR process utilizes criticism to enhance the process going forward. It does not require nor support punitive actions as a result of self-evaluation or external review. The sole purpose of self-reflection and any external review is to improve the PIR process, thereby increasing the likelihood of sustaining organizational long-term viability.

Social setting literacy is important to a PIR leader. Developing social settings for an intended organizational purpose has always been an important leadership skill. The PIR process looks at social settings as an important area to obtain potential implication information. Social settings in the PIR process allow members of the team an opportunity to sense changes in societal feelings and attitudes. These feelings and attitudinal shifts provide potential clues necessary to the PIR process.

Social settings in the mind of a leader from 20 years ago might be limited to cocktail parties and chamber mixers. As the rate of change has escalated, the social settings of new employees are clearly different from those in the past. Social settings today include online communities such as Facebook and MySpace. These social settings provide a host of information and can allow individuals separated by miles to be included in a community linked by a common interest. The leader of a PIR organization needs to be aware of the many different social settings that exist today and embrace engagement in all of the communities.

Communication is the most difficult skill to master. This skill becomes of greater importance in the PIR process. It is necessary to reach individuals in the medium in which they are comfortable. For communications, this means setting up a communications matrix that meets the needs of all those involved in the PIR process. Communications through multiple outlets, such as web portals, e-mail, newsletters, blogs, and so forth, may all be needed to keep the PIR process in place. If they are properly maintained, the likelihood of long-term viability is enhanced.

Communication also involves leaders being present, visible, and available for discussion with the participants involved in the process. Communication is verbal (spoken and written) and nonverbal. It needs to be practiced by organizational leaders and encouraged by PIR members.

Idea enhancement is the concept that all ideas are based on some organizational implication. An idea cannot be summarily dismissed by the leader in the PIR process. The leader is required to acknowledge the idea and run it through the PIR process. All ideas have merit. The PIR process determines whether the idea is an implication and classifies it as an internal or external impact that may be an impediment or an improvement to the organization.

Ideas being brought forth are the engine that drives PIR; no one should be discouraged by having an idea summarily dismissed before full review. If this situation occurs, the likelihood of missing a future implication is enhanced because that same individual will not feel confident in bringing ideas forward in the future.

These skills are the essential skills to focus on when employing the PIR process. Training to enhance these skills may be necessary for leadership before implementation of the PIR process. Adequate time needs to be devoted to skill enhancement so that PIR is an effective tool in enhancing long-term viability.

## NOTES

1. Tamara Erickson, "Global Generation X: Growing Up Between 1960 to 1980 Left a Tangible Imprint," *Diversity Executive*, May/June 2010, 12.

2. "Generational Differences: Myths and Realities," *Workplace Visions*, No. 4, 2007, 1–8.

3. Diane Thielfoldt and Devon Scheef, "Generation X and the Millennials: What You Need to Know About Mentoring the New Generations," *Law Practice Today*, http://www.abanet.org/lpm/lpt/articles/mgt08044.html.

4. Kathryn Tyler, "The Tethered Generation," *HR Magazine,* May 2007, 41–46.

5. Seth Brown, "Line Between Home, Work Will Blur More," *USA Today,* February 8, 2010, 11B.

6. Thielfoldt and Scheef, "Generation X and the Millennials."

7. Greg Hammill, "Mixing and Managing Four Generations of Employees," *FDU Magazine Online,* Winter/Spring 2005, http://www.fdu.edu/newspubs/magazine/05ws/generations.htm.

8. Tyler, "The Tethered Generation."

# Part II

## DECONSTRUCTING DECISION MAKING

# 4

# Reviewing the Long-Term Strategic Planning Process

To understand the reasons for utilizing PIR, it is important to understand how long-term strategic planning is currently utilized. We can accomplish this through a look at the entire process. While there may be slight differences in the planning process from organization to organization, it remains relatively unchanged overall. This is true in all organizations, including school districts, government agencies, not-for-profits, and businesses. The strategic planning process usually progresses through four stages: analysis, formulation, implementation, and control. It is important to work through the process to gain a sustained, competitive advantage. Unlike other types of planning, strategic planning incorporates the element of competition. It outlines how the company, agency, school district, and so on, competes. That might not seem apparent in the case of a school district, but it becomes clearer when you consider parents' choice of one school district over another through their selection of a residence.

The strategic planning process is how the organization creates value through an analysis of the strengths and weaknesses. In addition, opportunities and threats in the competitive battlefield are illuminated by *environmental scanning*, the constant assessment of the organization's competitive position.

Strategic planning ultimately strives to create synergy, a fit of all the systems and subsystems in the organization to work toward one end: particularized organizational goals. Strategic plans typically cover a period of 3 to 5 years. These plans are often initiated by the organizational leaders and almost certainly occur after a change in leadership. They may be required by regulation or rule, as in school districts, or they may be requested by the board of directors to help chart the future of the organization. In most cases, the strategic planning process requires the involvement of multiple groups of stakeholders.

The first step in the strategic planning process is to identify key individuals with a vested interest in the organization so that a steering committee can be empowered. The stakeholders in the organization often include management employees and representatives from the various departments. Individuals representing labor unions, if the organization is a union shop, are also invited to attend. Finally, representatives from the board of directors, customers, and regulators may be invited to the steering committee. The first committee meeting revolves around planning the process.

The first agenda item is typically developing a timeline, especially if required by regulation. Second, subcommittees are created to work on specific areas of the plan. Finally, guidelines are developed for membership of the various subcommittees. This might require developing a procedure so that each subcommittee chair can select their committee members.

The second stage of the planning process is the development of a mission and vision statement. These statements tend to be more open and less prescriptive in their construction. In the analysis phase, an attempt is made to answer the question "What is our reason for existence?" This is Phase 1 of developing the mission statement and can be a very difficult and time-consuming question to answer. It begins by analyzing where the organization is in terms of its business, why the organization is what it is, and what its purpose is. Trader Joe's, for example, does an excellent job at answering that question:

> At Trader Joe's, our mission is to bring our customers the best food and beverage values that they can find anywhere and to provide them with the information required for informed buying decisions. We provide these with a dedication to the highest quality of customer satisfaction delivered with a sense of warmth, friendliness, fun, individual pride and company spirit.[1]

Note that Trader Joe's mission statement quite clearly describes its current purpose and the means that it uses to accomplish it.

Once the mission statement has been written, organizations often create a shortened message embodying the concepts within the statement. In other words, the mission statement is restated as a slogan around which employees can rally. While not strictly necessary, it often results in the likelihood that employees can recite the slogan and, because of that, be better able to talk about what the mission statement is and why it exists. Owens & Minor, a medical and surgical equipment distribution company based in Glen Allen, Virginia, does just that. Their mission is to

> create consistent value for our customers and supply chain partners that will maximize shareholder value and long-term earnings growth: we will do this by managing our business with integrity and the highest ethical standards, while acting in a socially responsible manner with particular emphasis on the well-being of our teammates and the communities we serve.[2]

Their slogan is "Delivering the Difference."[3] Employees can recite the slogan and, from there, be better able to talk about Owens & Minor's mission and how it results in their delivering a difference to their customers and supply chain partners.

Vision statements are futuristic. The question "What is our business?" is answered in the mission; "What will be our business" is the vision. This is even more difficult given the lack of a crystal ball, and it is even more specific to each company than the mission statement. The vision statement often includes a statement of that organization's values. Levi Strauss & Company has one of the most appealing vision and value web pages, which can currently be accessed at http://www.levistrauss.com/about/values-vision.

Following a clearly written delineation of the worth that the company places on its history and values, as stated on the website, Levi's vision is simply "People love our clothes and trust our company. We will market and distribute the most appealing and widely worn apparel brands. Our products define quality, style and function. We will clothe the world."

The vision statement lays out the future direction, or game plan, for the organization. Sure, the current financial health of the company assists in planning forward, but remember . . . financial statements often lag in time by as much as a year. Profitability trends, asset mix, and amount of debt that an organization carries all play a role in the development of the future direction of that organization.

The answer to the question "Which should be developed first: the mission or the vision?" depends on a number of factors. Walt Disney had a vision long before Disneyland was built.[4] Bill Gates had a vision of a computer on every desk. While that latter vision has not been achieved, it is getting closer to fruition.

Some organizations have neither a mission statement nor a vision statement. The mission—or what the organization is—is therefore conceived primarily on the basis of its operations rather than a process of determining what the organization is designed to accomplish.

An example of this is a school district. The mission of the school may be spelled out by its mandate from the state in what it needs to accomplish. The mission and vision statements, while steeped in regulatory requirement, may improve on how the mandated services are to be delivered.

These statements will be the guiding principles for the development of the strategic plan. These statements take substantial time in their development and offer insight into the organization.

Once the mission and vision statements are developed, the initial goal planning can begin within the organization. This process is typically done by the steering committee. The committee brainstorms ideas on how to improve the business. This process is designed to take bold ideas and initiatives and bring them to a forum for discussion. Ultimately, the steering committee will decide which goals are included in the plan and which are excluded. These accepted goals provide the basis for the completion of the strategic plan.

Usually at this point, each member of the steering committee is assigned one of the accepted goals, as the point person for that goal. The committee member becomes the chair of the subcommittee designated to develop the goal for inclusion in the final long-term strategic plan. The newly designated chair is often empowered to populate the subcommittee from a cross section of stakeholders in the organization.

Depending on the goal, outside stakeholders, such as suppliers and service providers, may be included for participation. The committee meets to review the proposed timeline and begin its first strategy session. The committee continues to meet until a set of measurable objectives and associated costs are developed. A system of monitoring goal progress is often included in the subcommittee's plan.

Upon completion of each subcommittee's work, the steering committee reviews the various goals with its enhanced plan that includes costs, objectives, timelines, and monitoring. The committee then needs to decide which goals and objectives to include in the plan and which to reject.

At this point the steering committee assembles the preliminary report and reviews it with key stakeholders within the organization. Feedback is considered, and the plan may be altered to address various comments made regarding the plan by the key stakeholders. The strategic plan is then finalized and sent to the organization's board of directors or other governing body for consideration. If passed, the plans get forwarded to any agencies that may require them.

It is at this point that implementation of the strategic plan should begin. Organizations typically fall into two categories during implementation: those that see the process as a regulatory requirement and believe that it is a formality and those that believe that it is a meaningful endeavor and believe in the process.

For those that see it as merely a regulatory requirement, the plans are often placed on a shelf and forgotten. They may be pulled off the shelf in 3 years when the next strategic plan needs to be developed. The other organization is the one that lives its plan. Such an organization tends to follow the plan and implement the goals through the completion of the objectives within the timeline suggested.

Regardless of organization type, there is still no guarantee that the long-term viability of the organization has improved through the development of a strategic plan. One would think that the organization that fully embraces the long-term plan would have a better chance at long-term viability. The question to be determined is whether it is true.

## NOTES

1. Arthur Thompson, A. J. Strickland, and John Gamble, *Crafting and Executing Strategy* (McGraw-Hill, 2010), 28.

2. Owens & Minor mission statement, http://www.missionstatements.com/fortune_500_mission_statements.html.

3. Owens & Minor vision statement, http://www.missionstatements.com/fortune_500_mission_statements.html.

4. "Company History," Walt Disney Company, http://corporate.disney.go.com/corporate/complete_history_2.html.

# 5

## Deconstructing the Process to Demonstrate the Fallacy

**O**rganizations often complete strategic plans to help focus their efforts. To develop these plans, a commitment of labor and other resources is typically required. Once completed, the timeline covered by these plans is often 3 to 5 years.

When a strategic plan is in process, it is often monitored for goal and objective completion. Leadership compensation within the organization is often tied to completion of the goals set up in the long-term plan. The theory is that completion of the goals and objectives will ensure the successful continuation of the organization. Once again, this process is present in all types of organizations, including school districts, government agencies, not-for-profits, and public and private companies.

For example, Avistar Communications' compensation philosophy states,

> The Company's philosophy in setting its compensation policies for executive officers is to maximize stockholder value over time. The primary goal of the Company's executive compensation program, therefore, is to closely align the interests of the executive officers with those of the Company's stockholders.
>
> To achieve this goal, the Company attempts to (i) offer compensation opportunities that attract and retain executives whose abilities are critical to the long-term success of the Company, motivate individuals to perform at their highest level and reward outstanding achievement, (ii) maintain a portion of the executive's total compensation at risk, tied to achieve-

ment of financial, organizational and management performance goals, and (iii) encourage executives to manage from the perspective of owners with an equity stake in the Company. To achieve these goals, the Compensation Committee has established an executive compensation program primarily consisting of cash compensation and stock options.[1]

In its second point, this compensation philosophy demonstrates the direct relationship between the attainment of the goals within the strategic plan and the executive compensation. The executive's compensation is at risk because it is tied to performance goals. If the goals are not met, the executive receives less compensation.

To understand where traditional long-term strategic plans fail, one must first deconstruct the process. In the process of deconstructing, we uncover an area of concern, which is then addressed by utilizing PIR.

As long-term planning is developed in organizations, stakeholder buy-in is necessary. To obtain stakeholder buy-in, consensus-building techniques are often used. Consensus building is the process by which stakeholder agreement is reached on a topic through discussion and idea merging and tweaking. This process allows those involved to feel a sense of commitment and ownership in the final long-term plan. If this is done well, stakeholders go above and beyond what it typically expected to achieve the long-term plan results.

This process of consensus building can often lead to the need for PIR. If folks have done an excellent job building a consensus-driven plan, then individuals want to see the plan succeed. This process may actually cause objectivity to be compromised. As the plan is put into action, items within the plan may no longer be relevant due to the nature of change, as discussed earlier. These planned action items, although relevant at the time that the plan was written, may no longer be useful from an organizational planning perspective.

Members of the committee, however, may have been so involved in building the plan that they cannot see a need to adjust the plan and want to simply implement the one that was developed. These plans are often implemented to the detriment of the organization rather than to the benefit of the organization.

The following Circuit City example illustrates this point. In hindsight, Alan L. Wurtzel—son of the company's founder, CEO from 1972 to

1986, board chair from 1986 to 1994, and vice chairman until 2001—
acknowledged that the lack of serious competitive environmental scanning resulted in overlooking the threat of Best Buy. In an article written
by Gregory J. Gillian in 2008, Wurtzel is quoted as saying, "At some point
along the way, we were too focused on making a profit short term rather
than building value for customers long term."[2]

Remember businesses such as F. W. Woolworth, W. T. Grant, Hech-
inger, and Levitz Furniture? How about Atari Corporation or Lionel Corporation? Bethlehem Steel closed its doors in 1995, and Circuit City—one
of the latest in a long history of strategic screwups—closed its doors in
2009. Circuit City may have been one of the most written-about companies for years, with authors touting its success.

Jim Collins, in his best-seller *From Good to Great*, wrote about Circuit
City as a gold medal company.[3] Collins continued praising the company
by writing, "If you had to choose between $1 invested in Circuit City or
$1 invested in General Electric on the day that the legendary Jack Welch
took over GE in 1981 and held to January 2, 2000, you would have been
better off with Circuit City—by six times."[4] Well, that may have been
the case at the time, but the purpose of strategic planning is for sustained
competitive advantage. It is not to strategize the business out of existence,
as happened in the case of Circuit City.

What happened? Everything wrong happened. The organization shifted
from a differentiated strategy to a low-cost leader strategy, back to a differentiated customer-focused strategy, all with dinosaur technology. They
diversified into side businesses not exclusive to their core. They dabbled
in banking to operate a private-label credit card, invested in a minority
portion of a used car dealership, and created a digital video disc rental
system called Divx that customers rejected.[5]

In selecting locations for expansion, management arrogantly believed
that customers would come no matter where they built. Management was
wrong. In an attempt to save a nickel, they ultimately spent a dollar in
their plan B approach to selecting locations not convenient to the consumer. Then, in a last gasp for air, they strategically shifted again, closing
stores and taking it out on their employees by either laying off their most
experienced or cutting their salaries and then hoping that they would reap-
ply for their jobs at significantly lower rates. An organization cannot do
that and hope to maintain long-term viability.

Just as Circuit City was widely acclaimed for its savvy in outsmarting the competition, Tweeter and RadioShack, the organization found itself being equally castigated for missing the many turns in the road.

As demonstrated in the example, organizations have failed even though they may have had long-term plans in place that were being followed. Their failure may have been caused by impacts both internal and external to the organization and not originally contemplated during the strategic long-term planning process. The example demonstrates the fallacy that long-term strategic planning alone is enough to keep an organization viable.

The acceleration in the rate of change within our society strongly suggests that long-term strategic planning is insufficient to address changes that affect the organization between the time that the plan is developed and when plan implementation is completed. In some smaller organizations, strategic planning in its current form is simply no help when considering the resources required and the rate of change. For this reason PIR is needed.

Smaller organizations survive by reacting to changes in the market. When small organizations decide to commit resources to developing a long-term strategic plan, they may be consuming resources that could otherwise be utilized in a more meaningful deployment. PIR is a system that can allow organizations to take advantage of strategic thinking through the use of short-term strategies that may provide a better opportunity for long-term viability. With limited resources and constraints of time, PIR is the answer.

What has been determined is that the acceleration of the rate of change requires long-term strategic plans to put into place a system that can be reactive to changes. These changes could not have been contemplated at the time that the plan was created, and so therefore, they were not addressed. To follow the plan in that case then invites the potential for organization failure.

In smaller organizations, the resources to create the plan are somewhat limited; thus, a major planning error may not be able to be overcome, because the resources needed to develop a new plan were already spent on the original plan. Errors may simply put the smaller organization out of existence. In both these situations, PIR is needed to address change in society, to assess the impact of that change on the organization, and ultimately, to react to the data as quickly as possible. Organizations that utilize PIR will have already committed the resources necessary to react to such new data.

## NOTES

1. "Avistar Communications: SEC Information," http://www.secinfo.com/dVut2.1Cq6.htm#1j54.

2. Gregory J. Gillian, "Circuit City's Strategic Miscues Added Up," *Daily Progress*, November 10, 2008, http://www2.dailyprogress.com/business/cdp-business/2008/nov/10/circuit_citys_strategic_miscues_added_up-ar-84216/.

3. Jim Collins, *Good to Great: Why Some Companies Make the Leap . . . and Others Don't* (HarperBusiness, 2001), 8.

4. Collins, *Good to Great*, 33.

5. Gillian, "Circuit City's Strategic Miscues Added Up."

# 6

## The Future Is Never Accurately Predicted

In long-term strategic planning, the goal of the plan is to chart a course for the future. The future is unknown. It is difficult to accurately predict success based purely on long-term strategic planning because of the rapid rate of change in society. This rapid acceleration of change makes the impossible task of accurately predicting the future even more difficult.

The only accurate prediction that can be made today is that change in our society will continue. As new ideas and technologies are created and discovered, the economic needs and desires of consumers will change. Change need not be restricted to technological advances. Change will occur due to other external events. Political agendas will change governmental priorities. Diminishing natural resources will cause societal unrest and challenge geographic relationships. Aging societies will cause changes in consumer demands.

The fallacy in planning for most organizations is the belief that long-term strategic plans can foresee substantive change in an organization's products and services. In most cases, the change planned for in long-term strategic plans will be woefully underestimated. This is not the fault of the team that built the strategic plan. With the information available at the time that the plan was created, most teams do a good job at addressing the needs of an organization. The problem develops when societal change exceeds that which was addressed in the strategic plan. In other words, it is impossible to accurately predict the future.

A good example of this can be found with the impact of the BP oil spill in the Gulf of Mexico. The situation has devastated many leisure-related businesses relying on the beaches for their livelihoods. Many of the hotel, restaurant, and fishing businesses have strategic plans. Many of those plans did not include provisions for a massive oil spill. On the other side of this disaster are opportunities for organizations to financially benefit from the incident. Many of the companies that will be needed to help clean up the spill will find themselves benefiting from the incident. Many organizations that could have benefited from this environmental incident did not anticipate it and therefore might miss the opportunity to help.

Additionally, the political climate will change, as will the dwindling of current resources needed to keep society satisfied. These impending forces will cause change, but the form that it takes is much more difficult to predict. Once these changes occur—and they inevitably will—the use of PIR will be required to successfully direct an organization.

# Part III

**PLANNING IN REVERSE**

# 7

## The I-Process

PIR is a process. PIR is built on the concept that long-term predictions of the future are often inaccurate. Based on this premise, PIR was developed to help organizations achieve long-term viability by adjusting their planning based on short-term implications. This process can help all organizations achieve long-term viability. The process of utilizing PIR is called *I-planning* (see Figure 7.1). It is called *I-planning* because the process is described using words that start with the letter *I*.

The process begins with *implication scans*, which allow organization stakeholders to bring concerns to the attention of the PIR committee. These concerns will be evaluated by the PIR committee as empowered by the board of directors or other governing body to take part in the organization's PIR. This committee is chosen and set up in a manner similar to a strategic plan steering committee described in chapter 4.

Once a preliminary evaluation has been done by the PIR committee, it is designated as an *impact*, or it is *ignored*. If it is ignored, no further action is taken. If it is designated as an impact, further evaluation is required. The impact is then classified as an impact of an external or internal nature. After this designation is made, it is referred to an external committee or an internal committee for further evaluation. In smaller organizations, there may not be a need for two separate committees.

Implication scan committees can be internal committees made up of members from the organization or external committees made up of members from outside the organization. An organization can have both types

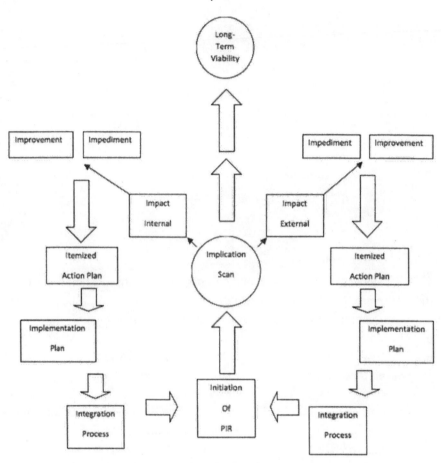

Figure 7.1.   I-planning process. PIR = planning in reverse.

of committees if needed. The determination of which type or types of committee depends on the effect of the implication on the organization. The internal committee should be made up of employees who deal well with integrating internal change—that is, the detail people. The external committee should be made up of stakeholders possessing the ability to take a big-picture approach to issues and deal with larger, external macroevents.

The real work begins from this point forward. The committee charged with the responsibility of evaluating a particular impact will begin to plan in reverse. The committee will take the impact and work it in reverse to determine whether it is an opportunity for *improvement* or an *impediment* to long-term viability. This determination will begin the development of the *itemized action plan* (discussed more fully in chapter 10).

Upon completion of the itemized action plan, the organization begins the process of *implementation*, which is the process of taking positive steps to correct the direction of the organization. If the itemized action plan was built around an impediment, then corrective action is taken to limit the effect that the impact has on the organization. Similarly, if the itemized action plan was built around an improvement, then appropriate steps are taken to incorporate change into the organization to drive long-term viability. Ultimately, PIR advantages organizations with an ability to harness increased opportunities.

Once implementation has occurred, the organization then begins the process of *integration*. Integration is the process of changing the culture of the organization so that the new change necessary for long-term viability becomes second nature to employees. Integration requires substantial work among leaders within the organization. Such leaders may not necessarily be managers within the organization. Leaders in the organization are those individuals who others look to for guidance and support. These individuals are essential to PIR and need to be identified by the organization early in the process.

As integration is accomplished, *initiation* begins. Initiation is the final step of the PIR process. Initiation is a process by which the recommended changes are put into place so that the organization heads in the correct direction. As this is completed, the entire cycle may be started again with another implication scan. This process is constant in PIR. It is the continual adjustment in the short term that improves the organization's chances for long-term viability.

To assist in visualization of the concept, it is helpful to imagine a highway with a cloverleaf interchange. At the intersection, there are plenty of choices. There is a higher level of distraction and confusion when one approaches the cloverleaf. If the correct choice is made, the planned trip will end at the desired location. This symbolizes the I-process. It is about recognizing in advance the choices that need to be made, selecting the appropriate course, and providing the proper direction to reach your destination.

In aviation, when an aircraft crashes near an airport, wake turbulence is often considered to be the cause. Wake turbulence is the disturbance of air currents caused by an aircraft moving through the sky. This turbulence can cause extreme flight conditions for an aircraft passing through it. PIR can be thought of as the process by which turbulence is converted from chaos and concern to opportunity for success.

Recognizing the difference between chaos and opportunity is not without training. The need for advanced preparation or a keen eye to address sudden change is essential. In taking this example to the extreme, consider what takes place when flying a plane. The National Transportation Safety Board, after investigating the cause of the American Airlines Flight 587 crash in New York on November 12, 2001, concluded that overuse of the rudder controls attributed to the accident. This occurred as Flight 587 took off on the same runway as a much larger Boeing 747.[1]

Flight 587 flew directly into the 747's wake, or turbulent air. The first officer overcompensated when responding to the wake, stressing the already highly sensitive rudder controls. In an effort to stabilize the plane, unnecessary adjustments dramatically shifted the rudder from one direction to the other in an overreaction to the air turbulence. Had the first officer resisted doing anything, the plane would have stabilized. A combination of three extremes contributed to the crash: overcompensation of the rudder controls, lack of training, and a design flaw.[2]

This example demonstrates how small adjustments made in a quick fashion may help alleviate disastrous events rather than making extreme adjustments. PIR is a process specifically designed to address issues of concern, regardless of their size, to help prevent "crashes" in organizations.

It is also possible to consider boating as an example of the PIR process. In boating, wakes can be considered an impediment or an improvement. Wakes are waves caused by boats moving through the water. In the extreme, wakes can cause smaller vessels to severely sway or even capsize; they can affect the natural environment, with plant and soil erosion due to the constant pounding of the shore; they can even cause damage to moored boats if not secured. However, if waterskiing or wake boarding is your sport, the larger the wake is, the happier you are. Boat owners intentionally add weight to the vessel to increase the wake!

PIR is a cost-effective way to plan for long-term viability in organizations. To properly implement the PIR model, a more detailed understanding of each component is necessary. The subsequent chapters provide the details necessary so that each organization will have the knowledge necessary for successful implementation.

## NOTES

1. National Transportation Safety Board Flight 587 aircraft accident report executive summary, http://www.ntsb.gov/publictn/2004/AAR0404.htm.
2. NTSB Flight 587 summary.

# 8

## Implication Scan

PIR starts with the implication scan. It is essential to the process that proper implication scanning occur on a constant basis. To accomplish this task, all individuals involved must have a thorough understanding of implication scanning. With the occurrence of proper implication scanning, PIR can be extremely useful in building long-term viability.

Implication scanning starts with an observation. Any observation, regardless of one's initial reaction, needs to be processed. Quite often, it is a stray idea, often dismissed as absurd or ridiculous, that leads us to recognize that change is required. The implication scan is the process by which observations are accepted into the PIR process. Observations should not be summarily dismissed simply because the implication committee thinks that they are silly. Much like a brainstorming session, all ideas have merit, and all are vetted in the PIR process.

It is easy to differentiate PIR implication scanning from strategic management environmental scanning. Environmental scanning involves searching the environment for important events or issues that may affect the organization. Environmental scanning is more futuristic. It does not look at what affects the organization today but, rather, what might in the future.

Implication scanning is observing all things both internal and external to the organization that could affect the organization. One may ask, "How do I know if a particular event will affect the organization?" The answer is simple: Any observation that strikes you as having an impact on the organization is an implication. It can be positive or negative; it could have internal or external change associated with it. The bottom line is—if it causes an individual to pause, then it should be brought forward.

It is helpful to think about broad categories when performing implication scans. Typical categories might include economic, technological, geographic, political, demographic, and efficiency implications. These implications may have a positive or negative impact on the organization. In every organization, there will be individuals who are more aware of certain categories than others.

For this reason, it is essential to build the implication committee, whether internal or external, with a diverse group of stakeholders. These are the eyes and ears of the organization necessary to perform PIR.

Economic implications are those that might have an impact on the organization based on potential financial changes. It is essential that economic conditions be monitored. This includes items such as interest rates, unemployment rates, labor rates, inflation, and other monetary conditions that affect the business. The key with economic implications is to develop the skill of scanning for subtle deviations that may lead to meaningful changes in the future. An example of this might be the day that George W. Bush indicated that home ownership was at an all-time high in the United States.

On a stop in Columbus, Ohio, on October 2, 2004, President Bush honored the National Association of Home Builders at the Greater Columbus Convention Center when homeownership was a prominent theme of the day. President Bush was quoted as saying, "Homeownership rates are at an all-time high in America, nearly 70 percent."[1] Bush continued, "To build an ownership society, we'll help even more Americans buy homes."[2]

In the same speech, President Bush called on Congress to eliminate a 3% down payment requirement for Federal Housing Administration–insured mortgage applicants in an initiative labeled the Zero Down Payment Initiative.[3] The statement would normally be viewed by most as very positive. As you read this book, it is easy to see how this one statement has implications that should have been planned in reverse by the banking and housing industry. Perhaps the economic collapse could have been lessened.

Technological implications are another category where implication scanning is needed on a constant basis. With the rate of change accelerating, as discussed in prior chapters, technology is playing an increasing role. Technology is advancing so rapidly that all organizations may be one technological advance away from extinction, without proper planning. Technological scanning is necessary to adapt to both positive and negative impacts.

Harnessing the possibility of technology is easier if PIR is used. It allows organizations a better opportunity at long-term viability. An example of the need to harness technology through effective planning can be seen in the diminished operations of Blockbuster Video and its failure to recognize the implications of technological change that allows movies to be downloaded to computers and on-demand television.

Blockbuster followed in the bankruptcy path of Hollywood Video, due to missing the turn in the road and failing to see what is immediately before it—namely, competitive moves, technological advancement, and societal changes. It is the same old story. In its heyday, Blockbuster and Movie Gallery (Hollywood's parent) looked to expansion as the only way to build a company.

Imagine sitting in traffic. The lined-up cars speed up and slow down, sometimes even stopping, depending on the volume, accidents, and so on. Both Blockbuster and Hollywood were looking far into the future or far down the road ahead of the traffic and missed the wreck immediately before them. Their plan of growth in stores and not in differentiation was so draining on financial resources that rebounding to capture a technologically advanced Netflix or RedBox (Coinstar's creative and convenient subsidiary) is now not possible.

Geographic implications can be local, state, national, or international. With geographic implications, the intent is to evaluate geographic disturbances or changes that may have an impact. A geographic implication may be a natural disaster. While it is obvious that everyone would be concerned with the welfare of the people affected by the natural disaster, there may be an opportunity to provide services from far-reaching areas if PIR is utilized.

Air travel and the Internet have caused tremendous changes in how services can be provided in remote areas. Minor disturbances to these systems can cause disastrous situations to occur in organizations with only a casual relationship to the services. An illustration of this effect might be the sighting of a road construction sign indicating that the highway will be resurfaced for a 3-month period. If the organization utilizes that highway as a main thoroughfare for shipping of products, then that implication scan needs to be acknowledged and processed through PIR.

A school district may need PIR for the road construction and determine the effect that it will have on bussing schedules and school start times. As the department hints at this information, PIR provides an active process to make appropriate adjustments.

Another example of a geographical implication—this time for a cruise ship company—might be a human-made disaster such as an oil spill in a particular region. This observation needs to be processed through PIR because of the potential negative (or positive) impact that it might have on the organization. The cruise ship may see business decrease in one region and so need to plan for an increase in another. Cruises from ports on the Gulf of Mexico may decrease while cruises in Alaska may receive increased interest.

Political implications are becoming increasingly critical to all organizations. In the global economy, it is difficult for an organization to operate in a vacuum free from political implications. As with all implications, political implications can be local, state, national, or international. A change in regulations may have an immediate impact on an organization. These potential impacts require monitoring for the subtle shifts of sentiment so that PIR can occur and the organization can properly plan for political change.

An example of this might be a state government looking to school districts for increased accountability. If that change in political desire is processed through PIR, changes in the business practices of school districts, including the addition of thousands of needed account codes, could be anticipated. Along with the additional account codes comes the necessity of additional employees to apply the codes. Proper budget planning can occur, and a true cost of implementation can be quantified if PIR is utilized in this situation.

Demographic implications are often ignored in planning but are essential to PIR. Demographic changes can drive entire industries. Everyone is familiar with the baby boom generation. Harry Dent has written extensively on the effects of demographic changes in societies, and the economic conditions that follow changes in demographics can have significant impacts on organizations.[4]

In the city of Reading, Pennsylvania, the population is changing. Failure to recognize the demands of a new population will have an impact on the organizations that exist and serve the populations of Reading. As these demographic trends start to emerge, PIR is needed to properly plan for the impact that it will have on an organization.

Grocery chains in the Reading area slowly recognized the demands of the changing population. The city initially had small independent community grocery stores that catered to the cooking needs of the Hispanic and Latino population. Not only did this diverse community expand to the suburbs around the city, but the style of cooking expanded, and the demand for more exclusive ingredients with which to cook increased.

Visiting the community grocery stores was inconvenient, but the chains did not initially recognize the demand for a greater variety of products. One local chain was slow to recognize the demand and concentrated a small line of products in one aisle. Today all the chains in the area finally have a fairly robust selection of not just ethnic foods but health foods, including vegetarian selections, catering yet to another population segment. However, if PIR had been utilized, it is likely that the chains could have responded more quickly to the changing environment.

As the demographics in Reading changed, so too did the marketing of most services in the area, including banking. To attract the population for whom English is the second language, the marketing focus of most service industries, including banking and health care, had to be adjusted by initially adding translators to recognize this large segment of the population. The question then became how to efficiently integrate the English-as-a-second-language silo into the organization.

This is also true for the Reading School District. As the population of the city changes, the needs to improve performance may need to shift. The shifting needs generated within the school system must be addressed. Reacting in an untimely fashion is to invite frustration and poor performance results. PIR provides a process that more actively pursues organizational adjustments based on observations by all employees. This includes teachers, support service workers, and administrators.

Efficiency implications in PIR can be a quasi-technology category. Efficiency is often linked to technological advances. It is a separate category because individuals who tend to work in a particular field often have difficulty approaching or understanding change as it relates to them. It may be necessary to look at organizational processes from a completely different perspective from that which is comfortable for individuals. Perhaps stakeholders from other sectors might scan departments for efficiency impacts.

This process allows individuals not constrained by their paradigm to force a review of a practice or procedure. In the end, PIR can help organizations become more efficient. The possibility is greatly enhanced by having a separate committee dedicated to efficiency implications. This category also tends to focus on internal impacts rather than external impacts, which allows a balanced approach to implication scans.

The primary purpose of the implication scan is to record the observation. Second, the implication scan is where the observation is categorized into an impact. The final requirement of the implication scan is to determine whether the impact will be external or internal to the organization. In other words, is it an internal change to our organizational process for success, or is it an external force that requires the organization to change?

PIR is a process that looks at an observation, works up its potential impact, and then reverse plans the event, affecting the organization to present time so that appropriate steps can be taken. It is not possible to successfully implement PIR if implication scanning is not done well.

## NOTES

1. Steve Zurier, "Bush Honors the NAHB During Stop in Ohio," *Builder*, November 2004, http://www.builderonline.com/null/bush-honors-the-nahb-during-stop-in-ohio-80329.aspx.

2. Zurier, "Bush Honors the NAHB."

3. Zurier, "Bush Honors the NAHB."

4. "The Dent Method: Economic Forecasting Based on Changes in Demographic Trends," http://www.hsdent.com/the-dent-method/.

# 9

## Impact Evaluation

The impact evaluation process follows the implication scanning and accomplishes two necessary tasks in the PIR process. First, it is utilized to determine if the impact is external or internal. Second, it determines whether the impact is an impediment to long-term viability or an improvement. These two functions are essential to the PIR process and must be completed in an earnest fashion and in a timely manner.

In small organizations, the same committee that accepts implication scans may be processing the impact evaluations. As is usually the case, organizational resources tend to drive the planning process structure. PIR is designed to be flexible and not limited to organizations or departments of a certain size.

In determining whether an impact is internal or external, there is the possibility that it may be both. In cases where the impact is both external and internal, the impact should be split into an internal impact and an external impact, and each should be treated separately. This is necessary because there may be different planning requirements for each component of a dual-impact evaluation. The same is true if the impact is determined to be both an impediment and an improvement. The process requires that the dual impact be split into two separate evaluations: an impediment evaluation and an improvement evaluation.

For example, societal changes such as eating healthy resulted in an external impact on fast-food restaurants such as McDonald's. Big Macs, while tasty, have a high calorie count. Health-conscious eaters know this but still like to dine at the fast-food restaurant with their kids. Parents today have the option to turn to the new menu items, which were designed to appeal to a healthier appetite but can still be purchased fast and for a reasonable cost, with both ideals being at the heart of the strategic drivers of McDonald's.

External change, the desire to eat healthy, affected the internal organization—namely, the choice of menu offerings. At first, this health-conscious population was viewed as an impediment. In this case, the organization reacted positively by creating tasty lower-calorie options, turning this impediment to an improvement. Ignoring preferences of a large and growing health-conscious population had the potential to negatively affect the bottom line. Instead, the organization continues to develop new, appealing lower-cost and lower-calorie menu items.

Upon the committee's completion of its determination of whether the impact is external or internal, the process by which recommendations will be developed is set in motion. An impact is external when the potential for change is outside the control parameters of an organization. External impacts can be from any of the categories utilized in the implication scans. The impacts are commonly grouped as external because the influence that they may have on the organization cannot be controlled by the organization.

An example of this might be a change in currency exchange rates between another country and the United States. In this global community that every organization can be part of, exchange rates can make the difference between long-term viability and extinction. If the corner bookseller prices its books at a certain price in euros for an eBay website, a certain level of profit is planned. The substantial change in the exchange rate could alter a profit or loss on a book simply because of currency fluctuations. The bookseller has no control over the exchange rate, but its organization is affected by the exchange rate change. This is an external impact.

Competition is also an external impact in which an organization has very little control. Cabela's or Wal-Mart's choosing to locate in small towns is a situation in which competition usually cannot erect barriers. Certainly, attempts at thwarting the opening of a "big box" mart have received David-and-Goliath acclaim but are rarely successful.

Internal impacts are those that are typically under the control of the organization. When evaluating internal impacts, one needs to remember that these can be completely controlled by the organization. Items of internal impact can be hours of operation, labor contracts, operations and processes, and record keeping. These are but a few of the internal impacts that might be controlled.

An example of this might be control of the hours of operation for an organization. The example of the bookseller can demonstrate this point. If the bookseller has the retail operation located in a certain area of town and has store hours from 9 a.m. to 5 p.m., Monday through Friday, the store will achieve a certain level of sales. If the hours are expanded to include weekends and evenings, it is probable that a different level of sales will be achieved. This is an example of an internal impact.

Costco and its hours of operation happen to be a good example of a cross continuation of analysis. According to Costco's website, the warehouse hours for all members are Monday through Friday, 10 a.m. to 8:30 p.m.; Saturday, 9:30 a.m. to 6 p.m.; and Sunday, 10 a.m. to 6 p.m.[1] In contrast, Sam's Club categorizes memberships between Plus, Business, and all members and extends hours accordingly, especially in the early morning, when it is likely that business shoppers will purchase products outside their own normal business hours. Sam's Club has early shopping hours for Plus and Business members and shopping hours for all members from 10 a.m. to 9 p.m., Monday through Friday. It has also Saturday hours from 7 a.m. to 9 a.m. for Plus and Business members and from 9 a.m. to 8:30 p.m. for all members.[2]

Obviously, Costco is less convenient to the Plus and Business member and for those who have a regular membership and prefer to shop on a Saturday evening. Has Costco lost the opportunity based on reduced hours of operation to attract the small business owner? Perhaps. Membership fees and location may also have an impact, but the question remains: In looking at corporate culture, is Costco more sensitive to the hours of operation based on a philosophical corporate direction? The answer is yes. In this case, an internal weakness, hours of operation, is also an internal strength.

Chick-fil-A is another example of a company that balances weaknesses and strengths based on company culture. The founders of Chick-fil-A keep the business closed on Sundays to provide their employees with a day of rest, regardless of the fact that many customers would like to purchase from Chick-fil-A on Sundays. The culture of the company is more important to the owners than the potential revenue generated from operating on the 7th day of the week.[3]

Overall, the impact process is not designed to be a time-consuming process; it is simply a categorization process so that the real planning work can begin in the PIR process.

## NOTES

1. Costco hours are listed for all warehouses at "Find a Costco Warehouse," http://www.costco.com/warehouse/locator.aspx?lang=enus&topnav=&whse=bc.

2. Sam's hours based on membership are listed for all stores at "About Membership," http://www.samsclub.com/sams/pagedetails/content.jsp?page Name=aboutSams.

3. "Closed on Sunday Policy," Chick-fil-A, http://www.chick-fil-a.com/ #pressroom.

# 10

## Itemized Action Plans

When the impact committee determines whether the impact is an impediment or an improvement, the real work of PIR begins. The process by which organizational issues are addressed in PIR is in the development of the itemized action plan (IAP). IAPs develop the assessed impacts into scenarios where each potential improvement or impediment is considered. Upon these considerations, a plan is developed that recommends action for the organization. These actions constitute the organization's best moves in addressing the concerns raised by the implication scanning process.

An IAP allows for the construction of a miniplan that is detailed and specific to an individual issue. It may be possible to have a series of IAPs being implemented at the same time. Some of these plans may be simple and easy to implement. Other plans may be more complex and require substantially more work and time to fully implement. In the end, it is these plans that develop a clear strategy for implementation. These plans allow change to be implemented and managed by the individuals in the organizations. Finally, these IAPs help to build the culture of change necessary to achieve long-term viability through the practice of experiencing change on an ongoing basis.

There are two types of IAPs that are utilized in the PIR process. The first is the improvement IAP, which recommends change that has an immediate positive impact on the organization. These plans are characterized by dealing with change that is viewed as beneficial to the organization.

The second type of IAP is the impediment IAP. This IAP is needed to address potential change that is detrimental to the organization. It should be noted that improvement and impediment IAP sheets can both have a positive impact on the organization. Each plan simply addresses a type of change from a different perspective. In the end, both are needed in the PIR process to improve the opportunity to achieve long-term viability.

Both the improvement IAP and the impediment IAP are based on the impact developed from the implication scan. Each will already be categorized into an external or internal impact. Additionally, each has been further categorized into an improvement impact or an impediment impact, so this process picks up the work at this point.

An improvement IAP is developed because an event has been detected that has the potential to affect the organization in a beneficial manner. An example of this might be a process that was handled by an outside contractor, but an employee within the organization now has the skill set to accomplish the task. The IAP sheet indicates the change that is necessary.

An impediment IAP is developed because an event has been detected that has the potential to affect the organization in a detrimental manner. An example of this might be a process that was handled by an outside contractor, but the outside contractor no longer provides the service. An alternative may need to be developed within the organization to accomplish the task. The impediment IAP sheet indicates the change that is necessary.

It is important to recognize that IAP sheets are indications of potential change necessary for long-term viability. Often, in any organization, when small changes that should be dealt with are ignored, the organization becomes diminished. It many cases, it is not just one small event that causes an organization to fail but an accumulation of change that goes unnoticed and is therefore not addressed.

IAPs bring these small events or triggers to the attention of those in charge of business planning so that a conscious decision may be made regarding the event. Ultimately, it is the designated leader in the organization who decides whether an IAP moves forward in the PIR process. Moving the process forward requires the IAP to move to the implementation phase of PIR for further development.

# 11

## Implementation Plan

Upon completion of the IAP, it is time to plan for implementation. The implementation plan is a key component to PIR. In the PIR process, implementation planning is where the costs and procedures are more fully developed for the integration of the change. In other words, this is where the organization needs to make a commitment to moving forward with the change item.

If the organization fails to commit to the proposed changes and any associated costs and training identified by the IAP sheet, the PIR process will fail. It is important that everyone understand that resources must be identified and plans developed to bring about the change necessary for long-term viability.

This is not to say that the planning committee is free from negotiating with organizational leadership. As is the case with most planning decisions, compromise or consensus may be needed to reach an agreement regarding how to implement change without bankrupting the organization. After all, the goal of PIR is the long-term viability of the organization, not an overstretching of resources that leaves the company at a higher risk than the failure to implement the PIR recommendation.

When planning for change, it is essential that the costs be fully considered. Costs include any material costs associated with the change item, such as software or hardware needs, equipment purchases, or purchasing changes due to vendor inflexibility. The costs associated with change items should be further broken down into onetime purchases and ongoing required purchases. It is important to create these two categories. It may be possible to overcome onetime costs through the use of an organization's capital budget, but a potential annual cost increase may be prohibitive to the organization's long-term viability.

Take, for example, the purchase of office printers. The cost of the printers—depending on size, capability, and number of employees using it—can range anywhere from $80 to more than $7,000 each. The cost of the printer, however, is not the only expense. The cost of ink cartridges must be factored into the budget as much as a ready supply of paper. Thousands of dollars could be allocated to the use and maintenance of printers. In some organizations, going green is not an option and, as a result, must stress the budget to purchase the necessary supplies.

The second component that must be committed by the organization involves human resources. Training employees on a new procedure can be costly. Quite often these costs are hidden because leadership fails to be fully informed of the impact on the financial bottom line of the true cost of training. Training costs include the cost of the training materials, the cost of the training professionals, and the cost to the organization of having their employees in training instead of working on their associated projects. All costs involving training must be detailed to make an accurate assessment of the change item.

The following two examples help illustrate, in a manner similar to the material cost changes noted, how costs of training can be calculated and therefore provide a sense of the significance of their impact on an organization.

The first example is fairly straightforward. A company makes the determination that outsourcing a function of an operation no longer meets the needs of the company, and it decides to return the function in-house. Training personnel would cost $10,000 per employee, which includes training materials and lost work hours. Multiply this by the five employees required to perform the contracted service, and the cost of training totals $50,000. Outsourcing the function costs $100,000. The efficiency on the change after initiation would be 50%, or $50,000/$100,000. Not a bad savings considering that the organization may want more control in its operations process.

What is not considered in this calculation is the expectation that better-trained employees may want increased salaries and responsibilities, which may further affect cost to the organization.

The second example is more complex. Consider the costs associated with training a special education teacher to write an effective individualized education plan. The cost of training includes not just the training materials ($1,000) and travel ($800) but also lost work hours, including benefits ($322 per day) and the cost of hiring a substitute teacher ($235 per day). For a 3-day program, the cost of training totals $3,471. Although an individualized education plan is a requirement for a special needs student, it is not a requirement that a school district formally train its teachers on how to prepare one.

The total cost of training teachers on how to write individualized education plans could be argued as an unnecessary expenditure for the school district. The hidden costs, however, are overwhelming. For example, the cost of defending the lawsuit that may be filed by the parents who believe that their child is not receiving the appropriate services would be prohibitive, especially when including the costs associated with due process hearings and so on.

That the true cost of change is fully disclosed is essential in the PIR process. PIR is about decision making based on initial information clues. The more information available, the greater the chances of making appropriate decisions that will benefit the organization. In the training example, the true costs are exposed for organization leaders, which in turn helps them make a decision on whether to move forward.

If the school leader chooses not to implement the change by choosing not to train the teachers on the implementation of individualized education plans for special education students, the cost may exceed the true cost just presented in the implementation plan. In other words, the potential loss to the school district from a lawsuit for failing to implement an individualized education plan may be far greater than the true cost to train the teachers in the appropriate way. With PIR, all considerations are on the table for discussion. Items in the IAP are priced, and training commitments in the implementation plan are received.

The implementation process also sets a timetable. This timetable demonstrates the committee's concept of a timeline for implementation or integration. The reason why this is developed at this stage in PIR is that it is nearly impossible to plan for implementation without information regarding resources. Once resource levels and training requirements are identified and agreed on, implementation can begin. In PIR, implementation occurs through integration planning. This is the next step in PIR.

# 12

## Integration Plan

Integration planning begins as the implementation plan is completed. In the implementation plan, commitments are received regarding the allocation of financial resources as well as human resources. With these commitments in place, the integration of change can occur. PIR requires integration planning to be completed where the "rubber meets the road." It is necessary to explain these proposed changes to the employees and managers who will be affected by the change item.

PIR requires that employees understand that they are an essential part of the PIR process. This might be from the submission of an implication scan or participation in one of the committees. This understanding might also arise due to an implication scan. Employees may realize that their jobs may be changing to help the organization achieve long-term viability.

At the integration level, employees are brought into the loop more fully—particularly, those that work in an area affected by the change. These employees become part of the integration of the change into the organizational operations. A discussion regarding the timetable, resource commitment, and accountability occurs at this level.

Integration is flexible. In dealing with change and the individual items identified in the IAP and priced in the implementation plan, it is important to recognize that some items that are truly necessary to understand may have been missed in the committee meetings. The lack of understanding of critical information may result in imperfect implementation and so give rise to the need for further change.

The information provided by first-line workers—those employees affected by the actual change implementation—may provide valuable additional information. Employees' concerns may cause a change or variation in the schedule in light of the new information provided.

It is critical that organizational leaders understand that first-line employees are a wealth of information. They are the employees who are tasked with performing any change designed; they clearly understand the nuances of the process. Service employees, for example, know what to accomplish to provide quality service.

Suppose that the PIR process recommends increased customer service by creating a more inviting environment for the customer, for example. Implementation suggests a shift from good to excellent service and requires the employee to not just greet but smile when acknowledging a customer. In other words, acknowledging a customer is no longer sufficient performance; smiling is the integrative suggestion.

Safeway Corporation, the second-largest supermarket chain in the United States, provides a real-life example of the just-mentioned smiling as part of its superior customer service program. Even though this example is from 1998, it was effective in sending a loud and clear message to employers.

As a matter of fact, blogging on this subject is still quite popular in 2010. Safeway required checkout personnel to smile and make eye contact with their customers as a means to improve service. Forcing a smile made some employees feel uncomfortable, and they voiced this as a concern to management, stating that some customers interpreted their smiling as suggestive.

Unfortunately, it was not until the employees filed grievances with their respective unions claiming that the mandatory smile policy created a hostile work environment that management finally decided to react. Had employees been consulted much earlier in the process toward what affords a superior customer service program, perhaps this public relations nightmare could have been avoided.

Many more examples exist with small and large organizations alike. What is cost prohibitive to an organization is when rank-and-file employees come forward too late with their suggestions or are simply ignored in the process altogether. Regarding the 2010 BP oil disaster, it will be years before the investigations, allegations, and so on, will be finalized.

It will be interesting to see how many employees familiar with the oil rig believed that unsafe drilling was taking place. Employees may have also known whether unnecessary risks were being taken, given the implication to drill in deeper water. Using PIR, the employees on the rig would have been consulted, as would have lower-level engineers.

Given an inclusive environment in which employees may participate without fear of losing their jobs if they dispute a change agent, alterations in the process can occur before implementation. The truth of the matter was apparent in a previous statement: The more employees are included in the process, the more likely they are to accept the change. As change items become part of the culture of the organization, they will no longer be feared. If PIR is properly performed and implemented, employees will recognize how valuable their input is to long-term viability and, ultimately, their success as continuing employees. This is to say that integration is the process by which change is accepted by the organization.

As the organization accepts these changes, employees integrate them into its daily operations. It is at this point when the change item has been integrated that employees begin to understand the impact that they have on the long-term viability of an organization.

Employees will more fully embrace PIR as the ideas and concerns that they raise are considered in the planning process. It is important for many individuals to feel part of something. PIR addresses the need for individuals to feel part of something larger, more powerful than just their jobs. PIR embraces this basic human need.

In addition to PIR addressing the need for humans to feel that they are part of something, PIR will trigger the bandwagon phenomenon. In other words, as individuals in the company who are skeptical of the PIR process begin to see change and recognition in a positive light, they will begin to embrace the PIR process. It will not take long for the entire organization to begin functioning as a team and thinking about PIR from a planning perspective. It is at this point that PIR will really begin to make a difference in the viability of the organization.

# Part IV

LEARNING IN REVERSE

# 13

## How to Retrain Strategic Leaders in the Planning-in-Reverse Process

The PIR process requires a change in the way that individuals react to an observation or a comment. Quite often, ideas or suggestions are quickly rejected as bizarre or impossible to implement. The potential advantage of listening to the idea or concept is lost and at times will end up being the downfall of the organization. To prevent missed opportunities and to plan properly for long-term viability, a change in approach is warranted.

An individual who makes an observation must be treated with respect. Even if the individual who is listening does not believe that the observation will have an impact, it must be brought forward to be evaluated. Even seemingly preposterous ideas may have merit. When the concept of telephone service without wires was first thought of, individuals did not believe that it would ever be possible. The same thought might occur when the idea of electrical power delivered wirelessly to homes is discussed, yet it may be within reach. History is filled with ideas that may have seemed far-fetched when proposed but ultimately became viable opportunities.

The phenomenon is best demonstrated by the historical example provided by the view that humans had of Earth. Everybody knew that Earth was the center of the universe. In proposing the idea that Earth rotated with other planets around a sun in a solar system, Galileo was in direct conflict with the Roman Catholic Church.

Galileo was tried during the Inquisition—an international tribunal of theology and canon law scholars charged with discovering and punishing heresy—and in 1633 he was banned from publishing his work and placed on house arrest.[1] This classic example shows how ideas that may seem preposterous at the time may indeed have merit and ultimately change the way that an organization or a community functions.

PIR embraces this fundamental idea that something completely different from what is considered the norm must be captured and cultivated. It is these observations that become the basis for long-term viability. It is important that training occur in any organization or department that plans on implementing PIR. To fundamentally change the way that people think about observations or ideas, an individual needs to retool the brain regarding observing and listening. Tom Peters, in his video *Radically Reengineering Business*, cites an example of Oticon, a hearing aid company based in the Netherlands, that was completely gutted and redesigned in terms of how work was accomplished.

According to Peters, in converting from a traditional hierarchical structure to a team-based operation, "it takes a weekend or forever."[2] In this example, Peters introduces a totally open office environment, with mobile desk units and cross-functionally trained employees. A total cultural shift occurred at Oticon, with complete employee buy-in. The key was communication. Employees had to listen, learn, and respond to one another. This is clearly unusual but not unique.

Another example of this is seen in organizations that wanted to improve quality and embraced the Six Sigma movement. Six Sigma was a unique concept when it was first proposed as a process introduced to improve efficiency and reduce error, with employees trained as Champions, Master Black Belts, Black Belts, and Green Belts in the organization. Training employees to the Six Sigma environment can take up to, if not exceed, 2 years.

When considering what there is for employees to learn, one need think about change and how modifications to anything are embraced in the organization. Chances are that change is not accepted readily. In proceeding with new process introduction, the new concepts are presented to employees; time must be allocated for the employees to come to an understanding of the concept and buy in to it; employees must then experientially learn the concept; and finally, they must be able to apply what they have learned. Misunderstandings can occur all along the way. This is exactly why employees require communication training. Learning to work together, team effectiveness, managing conflict, decision-making techniques, and behavioral simulation are usually skill sets that are part of the employee developmental design.

This retraining of team members is a critical step in implementing PIR. Individuals need to understand that they can freely submit observations for consideration and will continue to be respected by their peers. Regardless of the level of abnormal that is suspected in the observation, each observation submitted should be fully vetted.

## NOTES

1. Dava Sobel, "Galileo's Battle for the Heavens," October 29, 2002, http://www.pbs.org/wgbh/nova/transcripts/2912_galileo.

2. *Tom Peters: Radically Reengineering Business*, videocassette, produced by Jack Reed (1999).

# 14

## Understanding the Switch From Long-Term Planning to Long-Term Viability

The retraining of organization leaders and employees on listening and observing is the first step in switching from long-term planning to long-term viability. In long-term planning, individuals are concerned with charting a course into the future, which is developed with known facts available at the time of the plan.

These facts can quickly become outdated as technology advances and political, societal, or environmental changes occur. Decision making based on a long-term plan built in arrears will certainly require substantial alteration over time due to such changes. In other words, the long-term strategic plan will quite often look nothing like the original plan.

When an analysis of the long-term plan is completed, it frequently becomes obvious that the plan in its original form could not be completed. In fact, in many organizations, it becomes clear that if the plan were actually completed in its original form, the organization would be extinct. This observation can be seen in business, government, and schools.

The resources committed to completing a long-term plan are simply wasted since the plan does not benefit the organization as a whole and retooling must take place with more resources expended. PIR changes the way that one thinks about strategic planning. The focus becomes long-term viability rather than long-term planning.

Long-term viability can be achieved through constant adjustment to the organizational model and progression through the implementation of PIR. The goal of the organization is long-term viability; the course set by the organization is constantly being tweaked through the implementation of change from the PIR process. In this model, adjustments become the norm for organizational leaders, and change is the new constant, which allows for more responsive planning that will help ensure long-term viability.

If the nautical example of charting a course is utilized, the PIR process becomes much more clearly understood. For the cruise ship, the destination is a location. For instance, the cruise ship may be headed to St. Thomas in the Caribbean. The ship's destination is its long-term viability. To get to St. Thomas from New York will require constant change at the helm. The captain must steer the ship around storms, other shipping traffic, and through channels of appropriate depth. These adjustments are needed as the ship attempts to reach its goal. If these changes are not put into place, the ship has the potential to sink, and it will never reach its destination.

The information exchange necessary to complete the voyage is accomplished through an instrument known as the engine order telegraph. This device connects the master of the ship on the bridge with the ship's engine room. Information regarding the speed and direction of the engines is transmitted via the engine order telegraph. As observations from crew require changes, the information is transmitted, which includes moving in reverse (astern) or ahead (forward) at a typical speed, whether full, half, slow, or dead slow. This constant adjustment is a good representation of the PIR process.

As with this example, the destination of St. Thomas is similar to the new destination for any organization—long-term viability. The adjustments based on storms, traffic, and channel depth are similar to the implication scans that ultimately allow change to be integrated into the organization. As demonstrated in the example, this approach makes sense in today's rapidly changing environment in which organizations have to survive and thrive.

In a rapidly changing environment, it is assumed that fitness clubs will do exceptionally well given the focus of wellness, diet, and exercise across the generations. The *Wall Street Journal* ran an article referencing the closing of 1,000 Curves Fitness Clubs during 2009. Curves International Inc. was once the pinnacle of a new type of fitness fad, quickly catapulting it to the fastest-growing franchise with its 30-minute workout exclusively designed for women, in a women's gym, as managed by women. As quickly as it topped the chart, it now is plummeting in popularity.[1]

The recession took hold, affecting the ability for some to pay the membership fee, but more important was the claim that management did not listen to its franchisees and change the manner of operating the franchise. Two-income families with varied schedules simply cannot adapt to early-evening closing times. Society today is on the run. Gym workout, shower at the facility, and off to work is frequently the schedule for members. Curves, with the scaled-back operation, has no shower facility. It is also not equipped with rooms for dance routine workouts and other amenities that many of the more expansive facilities may have available.

Not only has increased competition challenged its membership fee, but Generation X and Generation Y grew up in coed dorms and coed gyms rather than in the women-only model of Curves. Exclusivity is not in vogue. From the Curves website, Curves identifies itself as "the largest fitness franchise in the world and the first to offer a 30-minute exercise program designed exclusively for women."[2] The company's unofficial motto, according to the website, is "no makeup, no men, and no mirrors," thereby eliminating a large population segment.[3]

Curves franchisees, according to the *Wall Street Journal* article, simply requested a change in format—staying open later and expanding facilities. The franchisees, being closest to the customer, clearly knew why they were losing members. An immediate response to allow franchisees flexibility in format may have been just enough to stay the customer exodus. Going forward, Curves may survive, but will it thrive?

This example strikes at the same chords as did Blockbuster Video. PIR would have provided an ongoing process for each organization to recognize and respond to the change in a manner that would have helped it thrive rather than falter and potentially fail.

## NOTES

1. Richard Gibson, "Curves Loses Stamina, Closing Fitness Clubs," *Wall Street Journal*, July 7, 2010, http://online.wsj.com/article/SB10001424052748704862404575351293938715632.html?mod=WSJ_Franchising_LeadStory.

2. http://www.buycurves.com.

3. http://www.curves.com/about-curves/history.php.

# 15

## Short-Sighted Leadership for Long-Term Viability

**W**ith an understanding of the importance of implication scanning from the previous chapter, it is time to tackle how this shortsighted approach works. Individuals will reach a point in an organization where they no longer feel threatened or embarrassed to disclose their observations. As these observations work through the PIR process, some will undoubtedly not make it to a change initiative.

These deletions should not be looked at as failures in the PIR process. Every implication scan is important. Those that do not make it through to the impact level are simply not worked on at the present time. In the future, they may become more important.

When implication scans go through the PIR process and ultimately lead to organizational change, recognition is needed. Individuals need to feel that their contributions are worthy and therefore important to the organization. Most individuals would rather receive recognition via acknowledgment in front of their peers. This process can be very rewarding for the employees and actually generate interest among other employees. As with all employee recognition programs, the top organizational leader should be part of the recognition program.

For the recognition program to really work, it needs to be unique, and employees must value the reward, no matter how large or how small. Embedded in organizational theory is the belief that money is not a motivator, but it can clearly be a demotivator if it is not recognized as being a sufficient reward for the task completed. The recognition program should receive just as much thought as the decision to enter into the PIR process.

One of the first decisions to be made regarding a reward is to determine if the reward will be individual or team based. This determination should be made while keeping in mind the fact that a well-orchestrated recognition program acknowledging individuals or teams makes employees feel good about themselves and even better about the organization in which they work. Much has been written about motivational theories and rewards. It is widely recognized in management theory that recognition programs can work if administered fairly and if the program fits with the culture of the organization.

If the organization values humor, it may be wise to embrace that culture when acknowledging good ideas. Good ideas could equate to something as simple as a light bulb trophy given to the group or individual with the best idea. That would be a humorous way to acknowledge contributions and incorporate the culture of the organization. The group or individual could be recognized at noon in the employee cafeteria, with the CEO bestowing the trophy on them and then inviting them to a private lunch in the executive dining room. The cost would be minimal, and the result would be priceless.

As employees recognize the benefits of participating in the PIR process, organizational leaders will begin to understand that PIR benefits not only the organization, through sustaining long-term viability, but also the leaders themselves, through increased respect afforded the employees, as well as that from the employees to the organizational leaders.

This respect becomes fluid and results in individuals discussing the new leadership actions involved in the organization. As outside recognition increases, the organization benefits from external respect. This external respect can often lead to increased sales and service contracts for the organization.

*Shortsighted* is a reference to an old derogatory term. If you were shortsighted, you were perceived as someone who did not care about the future or long-term health of an organization. PIR posits just the opposite—that a shortsighted approach is absolutely necessary for long-term viability. This is also seen when someone refers to a "Mickey Mouse" operation. The comment is intended to have a negative connotation, yet when one looks at the Disney Corporation, what is seen is a well-respected organization with a top-notch reputation. Apparently, organizations would do really well if they were Mickey Mouse operations. It is something that folks should strive for regarding comparisons of their organizations.

Let us look at a Mickey Mouse operation from the PIR direction. A Mickey Mouse operation is one that is simple, shortsighted, and of minor significance. The PIR process is designed for simplicity. Employees appreciate straightforward, honest discussions when change is incorporated into a process. The PIR process is shortsighted in the sense that the process is connected with the long-term viability of the organization.

A shortsighted approach tied to the long-term success permits quick turns in the road to preempt competition, changing consumer demands, and advances in technology. PIR may very well be of minor significance from the perspective of how intrusive the change appears to employees in the long run. Once employees have been through the process and trust and respect have been earned by employees, stakeholders, and leadership, the exchange of information is less intimidating.

A shortsighted approach is essential in today's changing environment. Smaller organizations cannot waste valuable resources on long-term plans that will never come to fruition. Long-term plans are based on items that will rapidly change, and the rate of change is increasing exponentially. This accelerating rate of change causes long-term plans to be outdated as soon as they are completed. PIR is the strategic planning model needed for today's environment. This system utilizes limited resources in a more beneficial process. A shortsighted approach is essential for long-term viability.

# Part V

REVERSE PROCESS PLANNING

# 16

## Developing a Realistic Timeline

In undertaking a transformation from static long-term planning to the PIR model, an appropriate timeline for implementation must be developed. The timeline should, above all else, be realistic. It is hard to pinpoint the exact amount of time that it will take to fully make the transition. It will more likely be several factors that determine the timeline (see Figure 16.1).

First, the size of the organization will play a vital role in the timeline. Often, smaller organizations or departments have a greater ability to adapt to change more quickly. This is typically a function of having fewer layers of administration or management, thereby allowing approval to be gained rather quickly. In addition, smaller organizations tend to have fewer employees, and those employees tend to know their coworkers much better than those in large organizations. This improves the level of trust and communications through informal networks, which can lead to increased efficiency.

Second, the amount of resources that an organization can devote to the implementation of PIR will have a direct effect on the length of the timeline. As indicated in an earlier section, the cost to implement PIR will vary from organization to organization. Some organizations may require new computer systems and devote dedicated employees to implement the new planning process. Obviously, the more robust the budget, the quicker the employees will be in acclimating to what transpires in PIR. This does

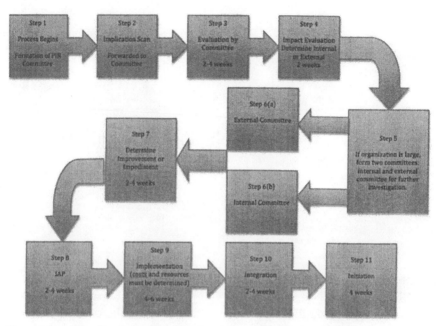

Figure 16.1.    Timeline for implementation. PIR = planning in reverse.

not mean that a great amount of capital is required; it simply means that it will have an effect on the timeline.

Implementing PIR can be completed rather quickly. To embed PIR in the organization so that everybody utilizes it, accepts it, and participates in it can take much longer. The process is easy for people to understand. Training takes little time with regard to implication scans. This is the level at which all employees can participate. In essence, it is their observations about events, news, and phenomena that are most important. The PIR committee that evaluates these scans will need further training. Training will be continuous within the organization to ensure that a rotation of employees is properly schooled in PIR.

The timeline for smaller organizations is approximately 3 to 6 months; for larger organizations, it may take additional time. Communicating the results of the implication scans is the key to ramping up participation in the PIR process. With any luck, your organization will be running PIR within the first year and seeing results immediately upon implementation.

# 17

## The Planning-in-Reverse Instrument

$P$IR is a process of looking at an event, statement, or phenomenon to determine the impact that it will have on an organization. The term *implication scan* is used in PIR to identify this occurrence. To more thoroughly understand the impact that the implication scan will have, it needs to go through the process of PIR. It is necessary to objectively look at the events surrounding the implication to determine the effect on the organization. All that is left is to determine how we reverse plan an implication scan.

The implication scan may be a statement made by an individual that strikes a stakeholder as interesting (or odd). To determine if the item will become an impact to the organization, the information surrounding the scan must be analyzed to determine the effect. Information needs to be acquired from a number of sources. Most of the information needed is readily available to individuals within the organization. This information determines whether the implication scan becomes a potential impact and continues being processed through PIR.

In years past, milk was delivered by the milkman to the doors of many homes. The dairy provided an insulated container that the milk was placed in to keep it cool until the house occupants woke up and brought it into the house. It was generally in returnable glass bottles. A grocery store did not sell milk. Eventually, an event occurred. Milk could be packaged in throwaway containers. This event provides an excellent example of how an implication scan is completed. Milk is now being packaged in disposable plastic jugs and cardboard cartons and sold in grocery stores.

An analysis of this statement provides clues to the potential impact that this implication may have on a dairy. The following analysis needs to be completed.

*1. Evaluate the statement for authenticity.* The first step in PIR is to determine if the implication that has been submitted is authentic. There are many statements made in many environments these days. Many of these statements spread quickly through electronic media. Some of the statements that people read and view may not be accurate. It is important in the first step to verify the correctness of the statement. Is this implication scan true?

*2. Are there supporting facts that bolster the implication?* The second step in the analysis is to determine if the statement is supported by reasonable facts. In other words, do the background data support the implication scan? Information may need to be investigated within areas not readily seen by the average observer. The formation of committees will help to objectively evaluate the scan.

*3. What potential effect will this have on the industry?* The industry may need to change substantially. Will your organization be the first to implement a change that is necessary for the industry to survive? Will this change provide a competitive edge for your organization? Could this cause the demise of your organization within the entire industry space in which you operate?

*4. Will this require a change to maintain viability?* Change may be needed to continue toward long-term viability. How must the organization alter its operations to utilize this potential impact in a positive manner? Even a defensive position from dreadful news can be utilized in an attempt to maintain viability.

*5. Is that change internal to the operations?* A determination needs to be made regarding the focus of change. Is this change an internal change? In other words, is this change going to alter the process by which the organization completes its mission? The determination of an implication as internal generally relates to operational changes that are needed within the organization.

Numerous examples exist of internal changes that affect operations. For example, initiatives to hire a physically challenged employee may result in an unanticipated increase in capital expenditures. Granted, the employer may already be in ADA/ADAAA (Americans With Disabilities

Act / ADA Amendments Act) compliance; however, additional accommodations may be required, such as the acquisition of a TDD (telecommunications device for the deaf).

Should an employer decide to hire temporary summer help, the Fair Labor Standards Act should be investigated before the hire of high school students to fill any openings. Internal implications—such as supervision, the number of hours worked, the length of hours scheduled, and the equipment to be operated by minors—may be a daunting challenge for an employer to be in legal compliance. Any changes to workstations, such as phone systems, new desk installations, and the purchase of computer screens, should be ergonomically correct to protect the health of employees. To do so may reveal hidden costs not considered when the initial implication was conducted.

*6. Is the change external to the organization?* Oftentimes, the implication impact is an external factor. A change in external forces that drive the organization may require substantial adjustments due to external pressure. These changes may require change to be implemented, but it generally causes the organization to change how it reacts to forces outside the organizational operations.

Any restaurant owner that has experienced nearby road construction has firsthand knowledge of an implication as an external factor that drives the organization to change. Road repair (external factor) either nearby or in front of the restaurant alters the convenience of customers to purchase food. The decline of customers prompts the restaurant owner to offer incentives to customers to entice them to drive out of their way to purchase meals. The incentives are often in the form of food discounts or coupons, which directly affect the restaurant's profit margin (internal factor).

*7. Is there a specific time frame by which this needs to be completed?* Time frames are often thought of in two distinct segments. A timeline may be imposed by the organization to implement change for the betterment of the organization. This type of timeline is set for organizational purposes and is not imposed by outside forces.

A bar, for example, that is marketing a "fresh" draft beer after the installation of a state-of-the-art tap system will impose a timeline by which the change should be accomplished. A retrofit to the existing tap may take less than a day. It is the preparation and training of personnel after the fact that adds to the timeline. Given a trouble-free retrofit, a 2-day timeline may be reasonable. However, if problems exist with the keg temperature or gas line pressure, the delay could be much longer as additional service personnel must be called, ultimately affecting the bottom line.

A timeline may be imposed by outside forces, which may set the timeline with little input from the organization. An example of this might be ADA regulations and deadlines in the building industry.

In an article written by Katherine McGuinness and published in the March 2009 issue of *Today's Facility Manager*, the author attempts to provide guidance to those managers charged with ensuring that ADA guidelines are met in building construction.[1] She explains that although the ADA is almost 19 years old and that the observance of the law is second nature for most facilities managers, current budget restrictions, among other things, challenge the practices of its compliance. Compliance seems to be a time-consuming, exhausting, and interpretive nightmare.

According to McGuinness, in addition to federal construction standards, there are state and local standards that are complex enough to daunt any facilities manager. Depending on the type of facility, claims McGuinness, facilities managers may have to comply with one or more of the following guidelines for their construction projects: the 1988 Uniform Federal Accessibility Standards, the 1991 Federal Fair Housing Guidelines, the 1991 Americans With Disabilities Act Standards for Accessible Design, the 2004 Architectural Barriers Act Accessibility Guidelines, and the 2004 Americans With Disabilities Act Accessibility Guidelines.

However, the new ADA guidelines, which were disseminated in 2004, are not enforceable standards until they are adopted by various federal agencies. As of the March 2009 article publication date, McGuinness points out that only four federal agencies have adopted the standards. Other facilities managers should adhere to the 1988 accessibility standards.

Could there be a more confusing regulation?

When these questions are thoroughly answered, PIR becomes effective

## NOTE

1. Katherine McGuinness, "ADA Trends: ADA Compliance in Difficult Times," *Today's Facility Manager*, March 2009.

# 18

## Training Individuals in Planning in Reverse

To implement PIR, individuals need to be trained to think in a new way. Leaders of the organization, in addition to all participating stakeholders, need to receive training. The training is less intense for the majority of employees. Most employees participate through the submission of their implication scans. These scans provide the basis for the real work that needs to be completed in PIR.

It is important to plan the environment when considering the training program. If financially possible, off-site locations lend themselves to an uninterrupted program. Inexpensive or even free locations may be secured at a local library or college. Training objectives should be clear to all participants. Selection of varied training methods should occur and be consistent with the learning style of the target audience.

For example, hours of instructor-led lecture will not be engaging for an adult audience that practices more hands-on methods on the job. Consider case methods, in-box training, simulations, or even game strategy to make your experience an effective one.

For these stakeholders who are already performing implication scans, training can be accomplished as part of the routine meetings held for employees. Employees need to understand the basic concepts behind PIR. In addition, they need to understand that nothing that might strike them as an implication scan should be ignored. The purpose of these scans is to create a pathway for events, reports, and items to be thoroughly investigated for possible impacts. Stakeholders need to know that all their observations are important and should be submitted.

For stakeholders who will be providing implication scans, the following points need to be stressed:

- All observations that strike an employee as interesting, odd, peculiar, or disconcerting need to be submitted.
- All implications scans need to be evaluated by the appropriate PIR committee to determine if there is an impact to the organization.
- The process needs to be transparent so that stakeholders can see the progress of a submitted implication scan as it is planned in reverse.
- All observations are important and should not be preliminarily dismissed or ignored and subsequently left unsubmitted.

The PIR committee members who take the implication scans through the PIR process will require extensive training. These individuals need to understand the following concepts:

- All stakeholders who submit implication scans are to be treated with dignity and respect. What might seem dismissible or ridiculous might turn out to be the beginning of a change cycle.
- PIR is a process; it is therefore imperative to follow the process and complete the necessary investigative work in an appropriate time frame.
- Individuals who are involved with PIR need to be open to all information and remove their personal opinions about the content of the implication scan to ensure that the data is evaluated in its purest form.
- Individuals need to be trained in informational access techniques so that each implication scan is evaluated via facts instead of assumptions.
- Communication skills need to be practiced so that the free exchange of opposing ideas or concerns can be evaluated and discussed in a civil manner. It is important to remain friendly to one another and understand that everybody's goal should be the long-term viability of the organization.
- Team-building exercises should be utilized so that the PIR team members begin to trust one another through an understanding of

everyone's strengths and weaknesses. The purpose of the exercise is to make the team work together better. Solving problems together is the best method to improve communication, decision making, and personal interactions. Rather than focus on the work at hand, the initial team-building exercises should be fun icebreaker activities. A good example is to present a problem such as building a tower of gum drops and toothpicks in silence. The fun element is when teams compete against one another to build the tallest tower for a prize. Candy bars work well as prizes. More serious exercises focus on case methods or simulations. Teams analyze the case at hand, for example, and form a course of action. Teams then must form one large group and arrive at a consensus. Compromise, factual justification, negotiation, and conflict are themes emphasized during the experience.

Training stakeholders to work as a team and to accept no statement as factually accurate until it is verified will greatly improve long-term viability through the implementation of the PIR process. A weekend seminar with few distractions may be the best environment to accomplish the training necessary to implement PIR.

# 19

## Ongoing Monitoring of Planning in Reverse

As implication scans are submitted for PIR, a system is needed to track their progress. This tracking is necessary because for PIR to work, stakeholders must be able to readily access the information so that the committee can follow the progress of each implication scan. This tracking provides two essential components of PIR. First, it helps create the culture necessary for PIR to work. Stakeholders will feel like their input is being taken seriously because it can be viewed by all with status updates. Second, it provides support demonstrating that organizational leadership is taking steps to help ensure long-term viability.

Organizational leaders need to demonstrate to interested parties that they are competent to lead the organization as they navigate into the future. This second important function of the PIR monitoring process allows interested parties such as banks and potential customers a glimpse into the proactive approach taken by the organization. A loan officer might be more inclined to maintain or even expand a line of credit if a demonstrable approach can be seen regarding the management of change. This process shows a path to long-term viability, and the monitoring of the progress is crucial in building trust.

The PIR committee needs to monitor the progress and disposition of implication scans. They can be tracked in a simple format for small organizations. A more sophisticated approach utilizing a web portal may be necessary in larger organizations. Whether through a notebook, a spreadsheet, or sophisticated project management software, monitoring of the PIR process is essential in determining the path of the organization.

A periodic check of the website PlanninginReverse.com will help individuals manage this new approach to organizational planning. As tools become available, they will be noted on the website. In addition, other important information will be posted on the website for use by PIR planners.

Constant monitoring and adjusting of the process is necessary for all stakeholders to adapt to change. Encouraging employees to make suggestions is an ongoing exercise for management. In the end, the key to the process is communication. We know this as a fact. The idea for this book began as an exercise in communication.

The business department at Alvernia University runs like a well-oiled machine — not because of structure but departmental personnel. This is not to say that the business faculty think alike. That could not be further from the truth. A more diverse group could not be found. The common thread is communication. Our departmental faculty talk to one another, sometimes loudly, all the time.

The environment in which the business faculty congregate is in a little office building on the main campus with a lobby furnished with a sofa and a few chairs. In this lobby, business faculty often just sit and talk. This is how the idea for this book came to fruition: One leadership/finance professor + one human resource/management professor + one department chair/law professor = a discussion leading to a new method of organizational planning, and a book is born.

The point is that the environment is one that invites, even encourages, employee discussion. This ultimately begins the PIR process.

# 20

## The Intended Results

PIR is a process. It is a new culture. It creates a culture of movement. It is an ultimate acceptance of continuous change. To achieve long-term viability as the intended result, an acceptance of the new culture is necessary. Organizations make this transformation at varying rates.

Organizations need to address the rapid acceleration of change. This acceleration has demanded a new way of thinking about organizational planning. PIR is a process to manage organizational planning in a more practical manner. Organizations should embrace this process and implement PIR at a pace acceptable to leadership. The implementation timeline varies depending on the unique culture of each organization. The industries or service sectors in which they operate will also have an influence on the implementation timeline.

Of particular concern is the significant change that school systems are beginning to experience. As the gap between households with children and retirees continues to grow, the fight for resources will require substantial change in the way that education is delivered. PIR may give school systems an advantage when it comes to recognizing and adjusting to the new environment.

Organizations that have been around for a long time may be less likely to aggressively move toward PIR. These organizations may also be the very organizations that need it the most. Organizations that feel complacent in their position within an industry or service sector may be missing the telltale signs of change. Quite often, the catalyst for change is a substantial attack on industry revenues or contracts. It is at this time that leadership realizes that planning has gone awry and needs to be drastically altered for survival. PIR may just help avoid these events.

So what is the intended result after implementing PIR in an organization? It is a change in the way that an organization thinks about its future. It is the acceptance of observations for review that might seem peculiar at first. It is the recognition that all stakeholders are important to the long-term viability of an organization. It is recognizing that change is happening and that the rate of change will continue to increase.

It is the idea that change is not a good or bad thing. Change is simply the environment in which everyone operates; therefore, change must be planned for as it occurs. PIR is the process to manage change, and long-term viability is the goal. It is the short-term responses to change that help achieve long-term viability.

Assume that the long-term strategic plan of any hotelier includes a message to continue, if not increase, the booking of rooms and for the guest to have a superior experience to spark return business and word-of-mouth acclaim. Corporate expansion is somewhere in the message. For example, the mission of Best Western International is "to enhance brand equity and increase member value."[1]

The rationale for focusing on this is found in Paco Underhill's book *What Women Want*. In the 2005 work, Underhill wrote that women under the age of 30 have surpassed men in earning power in the United States.[2] If corporate offices in the hotel chains do not recognize that women are making decisions about what women like in a room, where to stay, what to spend, and so on, they may very well find themselves behind the curve.

Underhill's research claims that women seek a superclean environment when they travel.[3] Some hoteliers, such as Best Western, have gone so far as to refit bathrooms with curved shower rods in their rooms.[4] This relatively inexpensive refit eliminates the shower curtain from touching the person taking a shower, thereby providing a perception that if the curtain touches no one, it is somehow cleaner. Following cleanliness, women consider safety, control, and a friendly, polite atmosphere. Ignore or chose not to act on the observations and risk losing business.[5]

Understanding changing demographics and how rapidly they can alter a large customer group is paramount in the PIR process. The old way of doing things requires meetings and multiple levels of decision makers to weigh in on a response, which can lag behind the competition. The PIR process theoretically takes an idea as simple as changing a shower curtain rod, among other things, and changes the perception of an up-and-coming demographic group.

By acting on ideas, no matter how small, rather than waiting out the strategic plan, an organization can take small steps toward futuristic leaps and bounds. This action may improve the chance for long-term viability. This is the PIR process. It requires a culture of listening.

## NOTES

1. "Mission Statement," Best Western International, http://www.bestwestern.com/newsroom/faq.asp?cm_mmc=SiteSearch-_-Search-_-BW-_-searchtool.

2. Paco Underhill, *What Women Want: The Global Marketplace Turns Female Friendly* (Simon & Schuster, 2010).

3. Underhill, *What Women Want*.

4. Meghan Cox Gurdon, "Buying Without Guys," *Wall Street Journal*, July 9, 2010, W11.

5. Underhill, *What Women Want*.

# Appendix A: Forms

```
+------------------------------------------------------------------+
|                                                                  |
|              PIR Implication Scan Form Worksheet                 |
|                                                                  |
|  Trigger or Event: _____  |
|                                                                  |
|  Date:_____                                    |
|                                                                  |
|  Description of Implication:                                     |
|                                                                  |
|  _____  |
|                                                                  |
|  _____  |
|                                                                  |
|  _____  |
|                                                                  |
|  _____  |
|                                                                  |
|  _____  |
|                                                                  |
|  _____  |
|                                                                  |
|  (Optional)                                                      |
|                                                                  |
|  Submitted by:_____  |
|                                                                  |
+------------------------------------------------------------------+
```

**PIR Impact Worksheet**

Implication Scan Trigger or Event: _____

Date:_____

Description of Implication Scan (Brief)

_____

_____

_____

_____

Impact Determination Discussion Points

_____

_____

_____

_____

_____

_____

Circle One:

      External Impact                              Internal Impact

**PIR External Impact Worksheet**

Implication Scan Trigger or Event:_____

Date:_____

External Impact Points

_____

_____

_____

_____

_____

_____

Impediment/Improvement Impact Points

_____

_____

_____

_____

_____

_____

Circle One:

      Improvement Impact             Impediment Impact

**PIR Internal Impact Worksheet**

Implication Scan Trigger or Event:_____

Date:_____

Internal Impact Points

_____

_____

_____

_____

_____

_____

Impediment/Improvement Impact Points

_____

_____

_____

_____

_____

_____

Circle One:

     Improvement Impact               Impediment Impact

## PIR Itemized Action Plan—IAP

Date:_____

Implication Scan Trigger or Event:_____

Impact: External or Internal:_____

Impact: Improvement or Impediment:_____

Summary of the I-Process Investigation

_____

_____

_____

_____

_____

_____

_____

Changes Suggested for Long-Term Viability

_____

_____

_____

_____

_____

_____

_____

**PIR Implementation Plan Worksheet**

Date:_____

Implication Scan Trigger or Event:_____

Impact Determination: External or Internal:_____

Impact Determination: Improvement or Impediment:_____

I-Plan Summary

_____

_____

_____

_____

Changes Suggested from IAP

_____

_____

_____

_____

Implementation Plan

| Item | Required Action | Cost | Timeline | In-Charge |
|------|-----------------|------|----------|-----------|
|      |                 |      |          |           |
|      |                 |      |          |           |
|      |                 |      |          |           |

**PIR Initiation Worksheet—Completion Report**

Date:_____

Implication Scan Trigger or Event:_____

Integration of Item:_____

Process Completion Report

_____

_____

_____

_____

_____

_____

Additional Feedback

_____

_____

_____

_____

_____

_____

Submitted by:_____

**PIR Implication Completion Report**

Date:_____

Implication Scan:_____

Fully Initiated:     YES     or     NO

Comments

_____

_____

_____

_____

_____

_____

Completion Date:_____

Submitted by:_____

# Appendix B: Education K–12 Example

I-planning example for education as described in *Planning in Reverse*.

## IMPLICATION SCAN

The governor of your state just signed a bill increasing the pension benefits of school employees. The new pension factor was increased from 2.0% to 2.5%. This factor is multiplied by the number of years of service and then multiplied again by the average of the employees' 3 highest years of salary. In addition, the vesting period for pensions was reduced from 10 to 5 years.

## IMPACT: INTERNAL OR EXTERNAL

A determination must be made as to whether this implication is external or internal. While every impact will eventually affect internal operations, the process is approached differently depending on the impact's origin. In this example, it has been determined that it is an external impact. It is an external impact because it was an impact originated by individuals who do not directly control the organizations that are affected by the change. The state legislature and governor enacted legislation that will affect every school district in the state.

*Determination:* Impact is external.

## IMPROVEMENT OR IMPEDIMENT

The determination of whether this is an improvement or impediment may depend on timeline and circumstance. For a school district that has a large number of senior teachers and finds resources scarce, this may be considered an improvement. The change may entice a substantial number of teachers to retire. Senior teachers earn substantially more than newly hired teachers, so a substantial short-term financial savings may be realized due to the new retirement bill. From the business manager's perspective, this may be considered an improvement.

From the curriculum director's position, the loss of a large number of seasoned teachers at the same time may cause student performance to drop; therefore, it would be considered an impediment. In addition, highly specialized teachers may not be available in the workforce at newly hired teaching salaries. These individuals may need to be paid higher starting salaries, thereby negating the financial savings associated with these positions.

As both sides of the impact are being analyzed, it is important to list all known information regarding the decision so that an itemized action plan can be developed. Often, these decisions may force the improvement/impediment decision to be split and dealt with separately.

In this example, the school district does not get involved in trying to reverse the decision of the legislature and governor. The time has passed for input if it is a new piece of legislation. The I-process is simply addressing the impact that it will have on the organization and trying to adjust to the new implication.

As discussed, the determination of impediment or improvement is more difficult than one might think. Ultimately, it will depend on the group making the decision.

For the purposes of this example, the impact of the new retirement plan will be viewed strictly from a financial perspective, so it will be listed as an improvement.

## ITEMIZED ACTION PLAN

The itemized action plan is where the real work begins. It is at this stage that a series of recommendations must be made regarding the impact. The itemized action plan should list the items that need to be adjusted or altered to maintain long-term viability. For this example, it might look like a series of statements.

*Item 1:* Determine the number of teachers who are eligible to retire under the new retirement plan.

*Item 2:* Determine the number of teachers in the available applicant pool to replace the potential retirees.

*Item 3:* Assess the number of difficult-to-fill teacher certification subjects that may need teachers.

*Item 4:* Assess the financial impact on the school district for the short term.

Notice that the education effect that this decision will have is not listed in the itemized action plan. The reason is that this example is based solely on the financial perspective. A similar impact that is internal may develop relating to academic success later in the year.

## IMPLEMENTATION PLAN

### Item 1

Determine the number of teachers who are eligible to retire under the new retirement plan.

*Action.* To complete this item in the plan, several steps need to be taken. A review of the listing of teachers regarding their years of service will help determine the number of individuals eligible for retirement under the new change. Since the pension system covers all school districts, years earned at other participating school districts need to be included in total years of credited retirement service.

*Cost.* When determining the cost, the reviewer needs to assess the cost of completing the action associated with this item. In other words, it is the cost of assembling the information that is necessary to estimate. The actual cost or savings due to this impact is calculated at a later step. Identifying associated cost with the itemized action plan is an important step in recognizing the full cost or savings associated with the impact.

The time estimated to complete this task is 3 hours. The payroll clerk's total hourly cost is $18 per hour.

*Cost:* 3 hours × $18 per hour = $54.

*Timeline.* The process requires that a timeline for each action item be established. Consulting with the employee required to complete the work will better enable an accurate estimate of when the work can be completed. After the payroll clerk's schedule was consulted, it was determined that the work can be completed in 1 week from the time of the request. Particular attention may be necessary to ensure that any changes can be incorporated into the regular annual budget timeline.

*Timeline:* 1 week from the time of request.

*In charge.* Identify the individual or position responsible for ensuring that the item is completed—typically, someone on the planning-in-reverse (PIR) committee. The employee who is identified to complete the work may be supervised by someone other than the designated PIR team member. It is important that the PIR team member understand that she or he needs to work with the employee's supervisor to make sure that the requested work is completed within the time frame.

*In charge:* business administrator (PIR member).

### Item 2

Determine the number of teachers in the available applicant pool to replace the potential retirees.

*Action.* To complete this item, a collection of data from several sources is required. A review of the current substitute teaching pool will need to be reviewed to determine availability to cover the potential subjects from the possible retirees. For the same purpose, a review must be conducted of applications from teachers and staff who have applied for positions but are unable to substitute. Finally, contact with the local colleges and universities to determine the number of graduates in certain certifications may be helpful in addressing availability potential.

*Cost.* The estimated cost associated with completing the action is based on current information. This work could be completed by a clerk in the human resources department, if the school district has one. If there is no such department, an individual familiar with the hiring process could complete the work. For this example, it is assumed that there is a human resources clerk capable of completing the work.

After the clerk was consulted, it was estimated that it would take approximately 9 hours to complete this assignment. The total cost for the clerk is $20 per hour.

*Cost:* 9 hours $\times$ $20 per hour = $180.

*Timeline.* In discussing the work schedule typically associated with the work, it was estimated that the clerk can complete the work within 1 week after the request is made. Work on this item, however, cannot start until Item 1 in the action plan is complete. It is a more efficient use of the clerk's time if the clerk knows what positions will potentially need to be filled before assessing candidate availability.

It will not always be necessary to sequence items from the action plan—in many cases, multiple action items can be completed simultaneously. For the purposes of this example, sequencing these actions is the best approach.

*Timeline:* 1 week after the list of potential openings is received, as a result of the work completed in Item 1.

*In charge.* For the purposes of this example, the human resources department falls under the direction of the superintendent. The superintendent has designated the human resources department manager as reporting to the assistant superintendent, who is a member of the PIR committee.

*In charge:* assistant superintendent (PIR member).


## Item 3

Assess the number of difficult-to-fill teacher certification subjects that may need teachers.

*Action.* Identification of the teacher certification areas or subjects that may be difficult to fill needs to be thorough. Information completed in Item 2 of the action plan will help assess this item.

A review of available teachers from the applicant pool, substitute lists, and graduation lists from colleges and universities is required to complete this task. A review of the information must be completed by a designated member of the PIR team to identify potential difficult-to-fill positions.

*Cost.* The cost associated with this task is limited to the time of the reviewer. In the case of this example, the human resources director will complete the task. After consultation with the director, the estimated time to complete this task is 3 hours. The total hourly cost of the human resources director is estimated at $50 per hour.

*Cost:* 2 hours × $50 per hour = $100.

*Timeline.* This task can be completed within 1 week of the request. Like the previous action item, this one is considered sequential. In other words, it cannot be completed until Item 2 is completed. While it will not always be the case, this action item depends on the completion of the other two items in the plan.

*Timeline:* 1 week after the completion of Item 2 is completed.

*In charge.* The human resources director is not on the PIR committee but reports to the assistant superintendent, who is on the PIR committee.

*In charge:* assistant superintendent (PIR member).


## Item 4

Assess the financial impact on the school district for the short term.

*Action.* The action necessary for Item 4 involves straightforward calculations. An assessment needs to be completed to calculate the total cost of the savings that the school district will realize per retirement. This will need to be offset by the cost of the replacement new hires needed to fill the available positions. The calculation should be made on an individual basis because the total number of actual retiring teachers is not known at this time.

In considering the cost to replace the teachers, careful attention must be paid to the information regarding the difficult-to-fill positions. Quite often, more difficult-to-fill teacher certifications require payment beyond the typical starting salaries. Another option is to try to lure a teacher in a difficult-to-fill certification area from another school district. The cost of these moves exceeds typical starting salaries and needs to be included in the calculations.

*Cost.* The cost to calculate the work associated with this action item is what is being considered regarding this item. The calculation can be completed by the assistant business manager, who believes that it will take 8 hours. The estimated cost for the assistant business manager is $45 per hour.

*Cost:* 8 hours × $45 = $360.

*Timeline.* The assistant business manager believes that this task can be worked into the schedule within 1 week of receiving the request. This request cannot be completed at the same time of the three previous action items. It is sequential since the information obtained from the previous action items is necessary to complete it.

*Timeline:* 1 week upon receipt of the information and request.

*In charge.* The assistant business manager has been identified as the individual who will complete the work. Since the assistant business manager is not on the PIR committee, the next-closest supervisor who is a member of the PIR committee was chosen to be the responsible party.

*In charge:* business administrator (PIR member).

## Summary

The summary of each completed action item is listed for use in the completion of the integration plan.

*Item 1.* The total number of eligible teachers in the school district was equal to 15% of the workforce. Our hypothetical school district has 200 teachers. Therefore, 30 teachers are eligible to retire. Of these teachers, 3 have been identified as difficult to replace.

*Item 2.* The applicant pool appears to be adequate to provide enough new hires to fill all but the most difficult teacher certifications.

*Item 3.* Three positions might be difficult to fill. Two dual science–math positions and one special education position may offer challenges to candidates with credentials.

*Item 4.* The total gross value of the savings from retiring teachers is calculated as follows: Thirty teachers at an average cost of $100,000—which includes salary, payroll costs, and benefits—is equivalent to $3,000,000. From this value, the cost of the replacement new hires is deducted. Thirty teachers at an average cost of $55,000—which includes salary, payroll costs, and benefits—is equivalent to $1,650,000. In addition, it was determined that the three difficult-to-fill positions will cost an additional $15,000 per position, for a total additional cost of $45,000. The short-term impact is summarized as follows:

| | |
|---|---:|
| Total potential eligible teachers to retire | 30 |
| Total potential savings of eligible retiring teachers | $3,000,000 |
| Less the cost of the new hires | $1,650,000 |
| Less the additional funds for difficult-to-fill positions | <u>$ 45,000</u> |
| Net short-term savings | $1,305,000 |

*A note on the long-term impact of pension changes.* The example does not include considerations with regard to the increased pension cost associated with the changes made to the pension system. We carefully considered whether an item in the example action plan should include the long-term impact of the pension rate increases. We chose not to include it, because it is not under the control of the school district and therefore not related to the retiring teachers.

The increased pension benefits may entice the teachers to retire, which immediately affects the school district. The increased pension costs associated with the benefit changes will need to be paid by the school district regardless of whether any teachers retire. The rate is set by individuals other than the local school board. In other words, the additional costs are unrelated to the implication. A separate implication scan to identify how the school district would deal with the increased pension cost would be appropriate.

## INTEGRATION PLAN

The integration plan is designed to engage the beginning of the implementation. It is where firm dates are put into place from the itemized action plan and implementation plan. The following information is relevant for the integration phase.

*1. Determine the number of teachers that are eligible to retire under the new retirement plan.*

| | |
|---|---|
| Start date | January 7 |
| Timeline | 1 week |
| In charge | Business administrator |
| Estimated cost | $54 |

*2. Determine the number of teachers in the available applicant pool to replace the potential retirees.*

| | |
|---|---|
| Start date | January 14 |
| Timeline | 1 week |
| In charge | Assistant superintendent |
| Estimated cost | $180 |

*3. Assess the number of difficult-to-fill teacher certification subjects that may need teachers.*

| | |
|---|---|
| Start date | January 21 |
| Timeline | 1 week |
| In charge | Assistant superintendent |
| Estimated cost | $100 |

*4. Assess the financial impact on the school district for the short term.*

| | |
|---|---|
| Start date | January 28 |
| Timeline | 1 week |
| In charge | Business administrator |
| Estimated cost | $360 |

*Summary.*

| | |
|---|---|
| Start date | January 7 |
| Completion date (planning) | January 28 |
| Timeline | 3 weeks |
| Estimated cost | $694 |

## INITIATION OF PIR

The initiation of PIR requires a considerable amount of communication. The announcement of the PIR implementation process is essential in letting the organization know of the proposed change. Included at this stage is the dissemination to all parties involved directly and indirectly in the process. Individuals who have work to complete are notified regarding their assignments. Individuals who are indirectly associated with the implication scan are apprised of the situation. The benefits of the change need to be clearly defined so that every employee understands why the change is being implemented.

For this example, the employees who need to complete research functions are notified of the start dates for their portion of the work. Also, faculty must be consulted through a separate meeting or through regular building-level meetings. Faculty should understand the importance of the change and the need to accurately predict the savings based on the current budget climate. Faculty may be asked to provide a nonbinding notice so that the administrators can appropriately plan for the hiring of new teachers. This information will be essential in the budgetary process.

It is at this point in the process that stakeholders begin to understand that each one of them has a stake in the future of the organization. As implication scans are tracked and implemented, employees will likely increase their participation in the implication scanning process.

Upon completion of initiation, a report should be submitted to finalize the effect of the implication scan results. For this example, the report may appear as follows:

| | |
|---|---:|
| Number of teachers who opted to retire | 20 |
| Total of savings of retiring teachers | $2,000,000 |
| Cost of new hires | $1,100,000 |
| Additional cost for two difficult-to-fill positions | $30,000 |
| Net savings as a result of the retirements | $870,000 |

In calculating the savings, it appears that only 20 of the 30 eligible teachers opted to retire this year under the enhanced pension benefits. Of the three identified difficult-to-fill positions, only 2 of the 3 teachers retired. As expected, the two remaining positions were difficult to fill and required additional compensation to attract individuals. The result of this implication scan was a budgetary savings of $870,000, which can be used for other areas of the budget or even fund a tax reduction.

# Bibliography

"Avistar Communications: SEC Information." http://www.secinfo.com/dVut2
.1Cq6.htm#1j54.

Brown, Seth. "Line Between Home, Work Will Blur More." *USA Today*, February 8, 2010.

Buy Curves. http://www.buycurves.com.

"The Challenge to Deliver: Creating the 21st Century Postal Service: 2009 USPS
Annual Report." http://www.usps.com/financials/_pdf/annual_report_2009
.pdf, 4.

"Closed on Sunday Policy." Chick-fil-A. http://www.chick-fil-a.com/#pressroom.

Collins, Jim. *Good to Great: Why Some Companies Make the Leap . . . and Others Don't*. HarperBusiness, 2001.

"Company History." Walt Disney Company. http://corporate.disney.go.com/
corporate/complete_history_2.html.

Costco. http://www.costco.com/warehouse/locator.aspx?lang=en-us&topnav=&
whse=bc.

Curves. http://www.curves.com/about-curves/history.php.

"The Dent Method: Economic Forecasting Based on Changes in Demographic
Trends." http://www.hsdent.com/the-dent-method/.

Erickson, Tamara. "Global Generation X: Growing Up Between 1960 to 1980
Left a Tangible Imprint." *Diversity Executive*, May/June 2010.

Fedex. http://www.fedex.com.

Freiberg, Kevin, and Jackie Freiberg. *Nuts*. Bard Press, 1996.

"Generational Differences: Myths and Realities." *Workplace Visions,* No. 4,
2007.

Gibson, Richard. "Curves Loses Stamina, Closing Fitness Clubs." *Wall Street Journal,* July 7, 2010. http://online.wsj.com/article/SB1000142405274870486 240457535l293938715632.html?mod=WSJ_Franchising_LeadStory.

Gillian, Gregory J. "Circuit City's Strategic Miscues Added Up." *Daily Progress,* November 10, 2008. http://www2.dailyprogress.com/business/cdp-business/2008/nov/10/circuit_citys_strategic_miscues_added_up-ar-84216/.

Gurdon, Meghan Cox. "Buying Without Guys." *Wall Street Journal,* July 9, 2010.

Hammill, Greg. "Mixing and Managing Four Generations of Employees." *FDU Magazine Online,* Winter/Spring 2005. http://www.fdu.edu/newspubs/magazine/05ws/generations.htm.

"Keynote Address by John E. Potter, Postmaster General and Chief Executive Officer, U.S. Postal Service 2010 National Postal Forum." United States Postal Service. http://www.usps.com/communications/newsroom/speeches/2010/pr10_pmg_0412.htm. April 12, 2010.

Lewis, Pamela, Stephen Goodman, Patricia Fandt, and Joseph Michlitsch. *Management Challenges for Tomorrow's Leaders.* Thomson SouthWestern, 2007.

Lundin, Stephen, Harry Paul, and John Christensen. *Fish.* Hyperion, 2000.

"Mission Statement." Best Western International. http://www.bestwestern.com/newsroom/faq.asp?cm_mmc=SiteSearch-_-Search-_-BW-_-searchtool.

National Transportation Safety Board. Flight 587 aircraft accident report executive summary. http://www.ntsb.gov/publictn/2004/AAR0404.htm.

Owens & Minor. Mission statement. http://www.missionstatements.com/fortune _500_mission_statements.html.

Owens & Minor. Vision statement. http://www.missionstatements.com/fortune _500_mission_statements.html.

"Postal Regulatory Commission Strategic and Operational Plan 2008 Through 2010." http://www.prc.gov/PRC-DOCS/home/main_nav/StrategicPlan.pdf, 4.

"Resilience: 2008 UPS Annual Report." http://phx.corporate-ir.net/External .File?item=UGFyZW50SUQ9MjA2MTB8Q2hpbGRJRD0tMXxUeXBlPTM =&t=1.

Sam's Club. http://www.samsclub.com/sams/pagedetails/contentjsp?pageName =aboutSams.

Sobel, Dava. "Galileo's Battle for the Heavens." October 29, 2002. http://www .pbs.org/wgbh/nova/transcripts/2912_galileo.

Thielfoldt, Diane, and Devon Scheef. "Generation X and the Millennials: What You Need to Know About Mentoring the New Generations." *Law Practice Today.* http://www.abanet.org/lpm/lpt/articles/mgt08044.html.

Thompson, Arthur, A. J. Strickland, and John Gamble. *Crafting and Executing Strategy.* McGraw-Hill, 2010.

*Tom Peters: Radically Reengineering Business.* Videocassette, produced by Jack Reed. 1999.

Tyler, Kathryn. "The Tethered Generation." *HR Magazine*, May 2007.

Underhill, Paco. *What Women Want: The Global Marketplace Turns Female Friendly.* Simon & Schuster, 2010.

Zurier, Steve. "Bush Honors the NAHB During Stop in Ohio." *Builder*, November 2004. http://www.builderonline.com/null/bush-honors-the-nahb-during -stop-in-ohio-80329.aspx.

# About the Authors

**Scott Ballantyne** holds a doctorate in education from Widener University and a master in public administration from Kutztown University. His undergraduate degree is in accounting and was earned at Alvernia University, where he is currently employed as an associate professor in the business department. In addition, he is a graduate of the Education and Policy Fellowship program, supported by the Institute for Educational Leadership.

Scott is also an award-winning teacher at the collegiate level, concentrating on leadership, finance, and school business courses. He was the recipient of the Christian R. and Mary F. Lindback Foundation Award for Excellence in Teaching. In addition, he was recognized by the Accreditation Council of Business Schools and Programs, which awarded him the Teaching Excellence Award for Region 2, which includes Pennsylvania, Delaware, the District of Columbia, Maryland, Virginia, and West Virginia.

Scott has gained practical experience as a Pennsylvania Registered School Business Administrator working in Pennsylvania school districts. In addition, he holds licenses for fixed and variable insurance and annuities and is a licensed registered representative in the financial equities industry. He has started and operated several businesses, including a retail business, a financial services business, a consulting business, and a charter boat business.

**Beth Berret** is an associate professor of business, with 21 years at Alvernia University. She has served on countless committees, including a number of strategic planning teams. Currently, she is the continuing studies business program coordinator and a member of the faculty executive team. She received a doctorate in higher education from Widener University, holds an MBA from Philadelphia University, and a BS in business administration from Bloomsburg University. She is also certified as a Senior Professional in Human Resources.

Beth is the recipient of the 2009 Advisor of the Year Award (Society for Human Resource Management Foundation) and the Saint Bernardine Award for Excellence in Teaching. Beth's professional experience stems from years of practice in human resource management, primarily in health care. She is a local and national member of the Society for Human Resource Management. She also sits on the board of directors and the Human Resources Committee for Berks Home Health Care Management in Reading, Pennsylvania. Beth is membership chair and a merit badge counselor for the Boy Scouts of America (Hawk Mountain Council). She currently serves as a division director and member of the Eastern Education Research Association and is active in the community. Beth is an avid animal lover and when not teaching, advising students, or spending time with her husband and three children, enjoys long walks with her German shepherd, Bailey.

**Mary Ellen Wells** is an associate professor and department chair for business programs at Alvernia University, Reading, Pennsylvania. She earned a bachelor's degree in accounting from the University of Massachusetts, Amherst, Massachusetts, and a law degree from Boston University School of Law, where she also earned an advanced degree in taxation. Before joining Alvernia University full-time in 2003, Mary Ellen was employed as a corporate and tax law attorney at the law firm of Bulkley, Richardson and Gelinas, Springfield, Massachusetts. In 2009, Mary Ellen completed a yearlong fellowship to become an Education Policy Fellowship Program fellow through the Education Policy and Leadership Center, Harrisburg, Pennsylvania. Mary Ellen teaches a variety of courses, specializing in various aspects of the law. She is a member of the International Academy of Legal Studies in Business, the Mid-Atlantic Academy of Legal Studies in Business, the North Atlantic Regional Business Law Association, the Eastern Education Research Association, the Association of Certified Fraud Examiners, the Northeast Association of Pre-Law Advisors, and the National Association of Pre-Law Advisors. Mary Ellen has published business law papers in the 2007, 2008, and 2009 proceedings for the Academy of Legal Studies in Business as well as in the *Business Law Review* in 2007. Her most recent article, entitled "Regulating Online Buzz Marketing: Untangling a Web of Deceit," coauthored with Robert Sprague, associate professor at University of Wyoming, was published in the fall 2010 issue of the *American Business Law Journal*. In addition to her professional endeavors, Mary Ellen enjoys spending time with her husband, their two children, and their dog, McCovey. They like to spend time at the beach, taking in the sights in major cities, and hanging out with friends.

# About the Cover

The cover of the book displays a replica of a nautical engine order telegraph. This device was utilized on ships to provide communication between the bridge of the ship (the command center) and the engine room. The device was used to send signals to the engine room regarding the direction and speed of the engines—astern (reverse) and ahead (forward), for example, in addition to a number of speed settings set as a fraction of the engine power, such as full, half, slow, and dead slow. It was with this instrument that the master of the ship (the leader) could get the crew involved in making adjustments so that the ship could maneuver through difficult seas and dangerous waters. Successful completion of the voyage was based on teamwork, communication, and the ability to adjust the speed and direction of the ship.

The master of the ship would order the telegraph utilizing the lever on one side of the unit. The engineers in the engine room would respond with the other handle to indicate what action was taken. The ship could not move in the direction desired if two-way communications did not exist between the bridge and the engine room. Ship speed and direction were completely dependent on the use of this instrument.

Planning in reverse is a process similar to the telegraph. The leader of an organization has to guide the organization in a particular direction. The leader is dependent on others to provide clues to adjust and change the speed and direction of the organization based on what may lie in front as a challenge. The approach of planning in reverse has been in use for years. It simply needed to be formalized so that all organizations can take advantage of the process. Similarly, the engine order telegraph did the same thing for early nautical voyages across uncharted waters.

16217622R00083

Made in the USA
Lexington, KY
11 July 2012